D1470218

# THE BELLWETHER

# THE BELLWETHER

*Why Ohio
Picks the President*

KYLE KONDIK

OHIO UNIVERSITY PRESS ★ ATHENS

Ohio University Press, Athens, Ohio 45701
ohioswallow.com
© 2016 by Ohio University Press
All rights reserved

To obtain permission to quote, reprint, or otherwise reproduce or distribute
material from Ohio University Press publications, please contact our rights and
permissions department at (740) 593-1154 or (740) 593-4536 (fax).

Printed in the United States of America
Ohio University Press books are printed on acid-free paper ∞ ™

26  25  24  23  22  21  20  19  18  17  16      5  4  3  2  1

**Library of Congress Cataloging-in-Publication Data**
*available upon request*

*To Mom and Dad*

# Contents

# ILLUSTRATIONS

## FIGURE

## MAPS

## TABLES

# Acknowledgments

While many provided me with invaluable assistance with *The Bellwether*, one person stands above the rest: Thomas Suddes, my former professor at Ohio University and the foremost authority on Ohio politics.

This project came together quite suddenly in early 2015, but many of the stories and concepts within it I discussed with Tom during the past several years over lunches and dinners across the state of Ohio. Most of what I know about Ohio politics comes from Tom: he is a great teacher, a great mentor, and a great friend.

Tom not only helped me develop the ideas for the book but also was instrumental in introducing me to Ohio University Press. I thank Press Director Gillian Berchowitz for giving me the opportunity to write this book, as well as the many members of the Press who helped produce it. I am honored to be publishing this book under my alma mater's imprint.

I also owe a deep amount of gratitude to Mike Dawson, who allowed me to use maps throughout this book from his excellent site, OhioElectionResults.com, and who also provided me with great details about the state's voting patterns.

My colleagues at the University of Virginia Center for Politics supported me in putting together this book, particularly Director Larry J. Sabato as well as Geoffrey Skelley, Ken Stroupe, and Mary Daniel Brown. I am truly fortunate to work with such smart and talented people.

There are many others who provided valuable insight into Ohio and national politics or who otherwise assisted me with the production of this book. They are, in alphabetical order: Alan Abramowitz, Alex Beres, David Byler, Mike Curtin, Jo Ann Davidson, Kevin DeWine, Brad Fingeroot, Joe Hallett, Brent Larkin, Henry Olsen, Eric Rademacher, Jeff Reed, Darrel Rowland, Jacob Smith, Bob Taft,

Sean Trende, Al Tuchfarber, Lottie Walker, Howard Wilkinson, Stephen Wolf, and Colin Woodard.

Any errors or omissions are my own.

Kyle Kondik

Washington, DC, February 2016

# INTRODUCTION

In their influential 1970 book *The Real Majority*, political demographers Richard Scammon and Ben Wattenberg identified the individual they saw as the American "Middle Voter." This person was a metropolitan "middle-aged, middle-income, middle-educated, Protestant, in a family whose working members work more likely with hands than abstractly with head." They then drilled down a little deeper: "Middle Voter is a forty-seven-year-old housewife from the outskirts of Dayton, Ohio, whose husband is a machinist."[1] Scammon and Wattenberg did not actually have a specific person in mind. Their description of Middle Voter was an archetype, but after the book was published, Wattenberg said, "I do not know for sure if the lady exists. But I suspect that if you looked hard enough, you'd find her."

And look the *Dayton Journal Herald* did. With the help of the International Association of Machinists, their investigation found then 46-year-old Bette Lowrey of Fairborn, a Dayton suburb located in Greene County.[2] Fairborn abuts Wright-Patterson Air Force Base and is the home of Wright State University, where one of the 2016 presidential debates was scheduled to be held. *Life* magazine profiled Lowrey. "She takes her sudden fame as Middle Voter very seriously," adding that she was "a registered Democrat who sometimes splits her ticket," and "is 'actually annoyed' by most politicians." "It's almost like being elected," Lowrey said of her status as the average American voter. "I must remember I'm speaking not only for myself."[3]

Every four years, Ohio voters end up speaking for more than just themselves, whether they realize it or not. While Ohio is not always or even often the single state that decides who becomes president of the United States, its consistent presence near the average national voting has cemented its reputation as one of the key states in presidential politics. Exploring Ohio's long history as a bellwether of the national electorate is the goal of this book.

Chapter 1 describes what exactly a bellwether state is, as compared with other terms, like "swing state," that the national press uses to describe key states in the Electoral College. It explores how the declining number of competitive states in close national elections has made the ones that remain, like Ohio, so important in 21st-century presidential contests.

Chapter 2 compares Ohio's record in the last 30 presidential contests to those of the other 49 states and finds that Ohio's overall record of voting for the presidential winner is the best, that Ohio is consistently closest to the national popular vote total, and that Ohio has provided the decisive electoral votes to the winners more often than any other state. After establishing that record, it's natural, then, to ask what is so special about Ohio, the subject of chapter 3.

This book's subtitle, *Why Ohio Picks the President,* can be read in two ways. The first is that Ohio voters actively select the candidate who is elected. In effect, Ohio decides the election. That does happen from time to time, and the state has found itself closer to the national average voting more often than any other state. But there is another, more passive, way to read it. The nation selects the president, and because Ohio has for so long mimicked the nation, the Buckeye State goes along for the ride. What's perhaps special about Ohio, then, is that it's not special at all.

*The Bellwether*'s middle chapters describe Ohio's political evolution from 1896 through 2012. Chapter 4 deals with the state's pre–New Deal voting record, which bears a striking resemblance to patterns dating back to the Civil War. Chapter 5 begins with the state's New Deal realignment, which really appears not in Franklin Roosevelt's first election in 1932 but in his 1936 campaign, an election that reoriented Ohio's presidential voting closer to the national average after it drifted fairly heavily to the Republicans. This chapter also chronicles the failed efforts by two prominent Ohioans, John W. Bricker and Robert A. Taft, to be a part of a winning national ticket, as well as Richard Nixon's long history of electoral success in Ohio.

Chapter 6 brings Ohio's presidential voting into the 21st century, while chapter 7 provides an in-depth look at Ohio's county-level voting and explores whether this bellwether state has a bellwether county. It also serves as an atlas of sorts of where the state's true centers of Republican and Democratic strength lie.

The conclusion offers some closing thoughts about the state's prospects as a reflection of the nation's presidential voting and explores how the state does or does not benefit from its place in the political spotlight every four years.

This book was written in advance of the 2016 election, when Ohio seemed yet again poised to play a major role in what could be another very competitive presidential election. But just because Ohio has been a bellwether for so long does not guarantee that it will vote for the winner in the future.

After all, Middle Voter and Ohioan Bette Lowrey looked like the exemplar of the American electorate in 1970. Yet in 1972, she voted for George McGovern, one of the biggest landslide losers in American presidential history. Ohio has spent the last 30 presidential elections, and others before that, generally voting close to the national average. But there's no guarantee that it will continue to do so, even while there's little indication that the quintessential bellwether is breaking away from the flock.

# THE BELLWETHER

# ONE

## *Swing States, Bellwethers,*

## *and the Nation's Shrinking Political Middle*

To a cynic with a good vocabulary, using the word "bellwether" to describe any aspect of the United States' political system must seem fitting. The term describes leading indicators or trends, and a "bellwether state" is a place that often votes for the winning candidate in presidential elections. But what does it actually mean?

A bellwether, traditionally, is a castrated male sheep (a "wether") that wears a bell and leads a flock of sheep. The bell attached to the bellwether tells anyone nearby where the flock is at any given time, and its lack of reproductive ability keeps its mind focused on the task at hand.

An impotent sheep leading the mindless flock through the dark? What a way to describe the states that pick the occupant of the most powerful office in the world.

That some states are more important than others in presidential elections is a consequence of the Electoral College, which chooses the United States' president. Instead of just a straightforward national popular vote in which the candidate who wins the most votes wins the presidency, each state is awarded electors based on the size of its population. The candidate who wins the popular vote in a given state gets its electors. As of the 2010s, there are 538 electors, meaning that a winning candidate must win more than half—a bare minimum of 270—in order to win the presidency. The

Electoral College winner almost always also wins the national popular vote, but there are exceptions: 1876, 1888, and 2000, for instance.

The *New York Times'* first reference to a "bellwether state" comes in 1948. "Missouri might well be the bellwether state for determining Presidential sentiment," William M. Blair wrote for the *Times* from Jefferson City, the Missouri capital. The state, Blair noted, had voted for the winning candidate in each of the past 11 elections. Blair suggested that at the time, in March, Democratic President Harry Truman's home state was leaning to the Republicans.[1] Missouri indeed picked the winner that year—Truman—by nearly 17 points in a nationally competitive election.

A related term, "swing state," appeared in the *New York Times* intermittently beginning in the 1930s, although the paper did not use that term (or another, "battleground state") with much frequency until the late 20th century.[2]

In 1960, the *Times* referred to Minnesota as a bellwether state,[3] and in 1976 R.W. Apple Jr., in a preelection guide on how to follow the results, cited Illinois as a bellwether that had voted for the winner in every election since 1920.[4] The Land of Lincoln backed the loser, Republican President Gerald Ford, over Democrat Jimmy Carter. Later years saw states like Pennsylvania, Oregon, California, Colorado, and, increasingly, Ohio receive the designation from the *Times*. For at least the past few cycles, "swing" has appeared far more times than "bellwether" to describe competitive general election states.

According to *Presidential Swing States: Why Only Ten Matter*, an analysis of the competitive states in the Electoral College, the proliferation of "swing state" is a relatively recent one. "The phenomen[on] of a state being labeled a swing state is largely a product of the media and recent campaign invention," Stacey Hunter Hecht and David Schultz argue.[5]

Bellwethers? Swing states? Are these the same thing? Sometimes, but not always.

## Defining the Bellwether State

Whether one refers to a typically competitive state in the Electoral College as a bellwether or a swing state, both seemingly have the same definition: a state that both is competitive in a close presidential election and reflects the national voting in a given election. But these terms are not really interchangeable.

Just because a state is close in an election doesn't make it a bellwether. For instance, Missouri achieved a reputation as perhaps the nation's most notable swing state throughout the 20th and into the 21st century, voting for the national winner in all but one election from 1904 to 2004, so the *New York Times* was right to flag it in 1948. The single time it voted with the loser was when it backed Democrat Adlai Stevenson over Republican President Dwight Eisenhower in 1956, picking the challenger over the incumbent by about two-tenths of a percentage point, making it the closest state in that election.

Missouri was a swing state in 1956, meaning that either side could have won it, but it was not a bellwether, because it was not representative of the national results. Not only did it vote for the losing candidate, but it did so in an election when the winner, Eisenhower, won nationally by 15 percentage points and captured 86 percent of the electoral votes. Four years later, Missouri was again a swing state—Democrat John F. Kennedy narrowly won it—but it was also a bellwether, because Kennedy's margin there was about the same as his national margin: he won both by less than a point.

Here, then, are definitions of both terms.

- Bellwether states reflect the national voting not only in close elections, but also in blowouts.

- Swing states can be won by either side in an election.

In competitive contests, bellwethers and swings are often the same states. In noncompetitive elections, they probably won't be.

The analogy of a wave is a common one in politics, with big ones indicating smashing victories for one side or the other.[6] Sean Trende of RealClearPolitics, a political news analysis and aggregation website, has a useful analogy to describe how this works in the Electoral College:

> Think, if you will, of a 51-rung ladder descending into a tidal pool. At the bottom of the ladder is the most Democratic state in the country. . . . At the top of the ladder is the most Republican state in the country. . . . The water represents the Democratic tide, driven by national forces such as the economy, presidential popularity, and so forth. As the tide rises,

increasingly red states cast their ballots for the Democratic candidates. As it falls, blue states begin to turn crimson.[7]

When that 51-rung ladder is assembled every four years—one for each of the 50 states and another for the District of Columbia—Ohio is typically right near the middle, winnable by either side so long as the national election is close. If a party's tide rises high enough to cover Ohio, history suggests that that is almost always sufficient to win the election. If the party's tide does not rise to Ohio's level, then that party's candidate almost always loses.

In close elections, Ohio is a swing state, but it generally is not when national elections are blowouts. For the most part, its voting patterns reflect those of the nation in elections decided either by few votes or by many votes. It's a state that can both decide the winner in a close election and reflect the nation's movement in a blowout. It moves the way the nation moves, and it has for quite some time.

## WHEN A SINGLE STATE DECIDES

The first presidential election in which there was widespread participation by average citizens—average white male ones, that is—was 1828, the year of Andrew Jackson's sweeping victory over incumbent John Quincy Adams. This was arguably "the first truly 'democratic' election, in that eligible voters participated to a degree not seen before."[8] It also saw the emergence of a true two-party system, even if it would take another three decades before both modern parties, the Democrats and the Republicans, would actually emerge (1856 is the first year both parties would face off in a presidential election, as they have in every presidential election since).

If the election of 1828 was "the birth of modern politics," as Lynn Hudson Parsons argued in his breakdown of the Jackson-Adams clash,[9] the first modern elections were not particularly close in the Electoral College. Take any state and its electoral votes away from any of the winners in 1828, 1832, 1836, and 1840, and that candidate still would have had enough electoral votes to win.

The first true electoral nail-biter, then, was 1844. While Democrat James K. Polk won with 170 of 275 possible electoral votes to Whig Henry

Clay's 105, the seemingly lopsided total is deceptive. New York, with its 36 electoral votes, voted for Polk by just a single percentage point, a difference of about 5,000 votes of close to 500,000 cast. Flip New York to Clay and, leaving all else equal, he would have been elected. "As stunned Whigs surveyed the wreckage, they quickly saw that the key to the election had in fact been New York," although "Clay, the savvy head counter, had known all along that New York was the key to the contest."[10]

That election marked the first of 10 times in the modern era (beginning in 1828) where the result in a single, closely contested state made the difference in the election. Those other elections are 1848, 1876, 1880, 1884, 1888, 1916, 1976, 2000, and 2004. In each of those elections, if the loser had won just one state he lost by a close margin (less than five points), he would have won the election. Additionally, in 1968, if Democrat Hubert Humphrey had won California and its 40 electoral votes (he lost by about three points to Republican Richard Nixon), he and George Wallace, the former Democratic governor of Alabama who ran for president as an independent conservative, would have combined to deny Nixon an Electoral College majority, throwing the election into the House of Representatives, something that has not happened since 1824. Had that happened, Humphrey likely would have won, because Democrats controlled 26 of 50 US House delegations. (When a presidential election goes to the House, each state gets a single vote, which presumably would go to the candidate whose party controlled that state's House delegation.)

So there's a long history of a single state making the difference in a close election. The nature of the United States' Electoral College allows for the possibility that a single state, closely fought, can determine the victor.

In a year with a big wave, states that ordinarily vote for one party will often vote for the other. States that aren't usually competitive turn into swing states, but that doesn't mean their results will look like the nation's.

Minnesota has the longest streak of voting Democratic for president of any state in the country (the District of Columbia's stretches back even further, but DC is not a state, to the chagrin of its residents). The North Star State has voted for a Democrat in every election since 1976, withstanding even incumbent Ronald Reagan's 49-state reelection tide in 1984. The state instead opted that year for former Vice President Walter

Mondale, who had also served as a senator from Minnesota, by less than 4,000 votes. Reagan won 59 percent to 41 percent nationally, but Mondale won his home state 49.7 percent to 49.5 percent. For simplicity's sake, let's round that up to a 50–50 tie, meaning the state was nine points more Democratic and nine points less Republican than the national average. Thus, it was still far to the left of the nation's center, and had Mondale not been a home-state candidate, perhaps even this reliably Democratic state would have voted for Reagan. Again, Minnesota was a swing state that year, but it definitely was not a bellwether. It was just that the Democratic wave in the tide pool, to borrow Trende's analogy, was little more than a puddle, so low that it barely colored even a very Democratic state with a favorite-son candidate's blue.

Meanwhile, the number of states like Ohio—the bellwethers, the ones that stick close to the national average vote in both nail-biters and routs—has been dwindling.

## The Archaic (but at the Time, Defensible) 50-State Strategy

Two days before losing an achingly close election to Democrat John F. Kennedy, Republican Vice President Richard M. Nixon campaigned in a state that had previously never cast an electoral vote for president.

On November 6, 1960, Nixon spoke in Anchorage, Alaska, completing an ambitious pledge to campaign in all 50 states. As he pointed out, "This is indeed, a historic moment. It is one that will never be duplicated. This is the first time in the history of the United States that a candidate for the Presidency of either party has visited all of the 50 States of this country."[11]

This was a promise Nixon had made in his convention speech in Chicago: "In this campaign we are going to take no states for granted, and we aren't going to concede any states to the opposition."[12] So Nixon visited places he would lose by 25 points, like Georgia: "I think it's time for the Democratic candidates for the presidency to quit taking Georgia and the South for granted," he said in Atlanta on August 26.[13] He would also visit Vermont, which would back him by 17 points: "Speaking to you here in the state, speaking to you particularly as a state that traditionally votes Republican, I would like to present the case for our national ticket, not just on Republican lines. That would be the easiest thing to do. I know that in this audience are people who are predominantly Republican."[14] Later, in the aforementioned Anchorage speech, he would proclaim that it made no difference: "As far as I am concerned, North, East, West, or South, it's all part of America and a candidate for the presidency should go to every state so that he knows what America is all about—and that's why I'm here."

Nixon's 50-state gimmick is perhaps one of the reasons he lost the election. Might his time in Alaska have been better spent in Illinois, Missouri, or New Jersey, states with more electoral votes, states that Nixon lost by less than a percentage point each? "All through the campaign," wrote Theodore White in his definitive *The Making of the President 1960*, "as the race narrowed and it became obvious that it would be won or lost in the teetering industrial northeastern states, Nixon was cramped by his public pledge—so that on the last week end of the campaign, as Kennedy barnstormed through populous Illinois, New Jersey, New York and New England, Nixon found himself committed to fly all the way north to Alaska, which offered only three electoral votes."[15]

As strange as it seems today to imagine a presidential candidate spending some of the final hours of the campaign in Anchorage, it actually was not so crazy back then. In their first elections, both Alaska and Hawaii were rightly regarded as battlegrounds. If Nixon's visiting Alaska was so foolish, then the Kennedy strategy was perhaps even more boneheaded: JFK made not just one, but two visits to Alaska during his campaign (the state went to Nixon by 1,144 votes). And while Kennedy did not visit every state, he did campaign in 43 of them, so JFK's strategy was nearly as nationalized as Nixon's was.[16] Maybe Nixon's mistake was not making the pledge, but instead saving a time-consuming Alaska trip for the end of the campaign instead of knocking it out earlier on.

Furthermore, while Nixon was the first presidential candidate to campaign in every state, candidates of both parties often campaigned across the nation back then. In his 1952 victory, for instance, Eisenhower campaigned in 45 of 48 states.[17]

A half century earlier, the populist Democrat William Jennings Bryan, by his own count, visited 29 of 45 states in his 1896 campaign, traveling more than 18,000 miles and delivering 570 speeches.[18] Republican William

McKinley, meanwhile, opted for a "front porch" campaign, staying put at his home in Canton, Ohio, and giving speeches to groups who visited him. McKinley's strategy was more in keeping with the tradition of the era, and while Bryan was not the first presidential candidate to give speeches across the country in search of support, the level to which he traveled struck some as unseemly, according to Richard J. Ellis and Mark Dedrick in an analysis of presidential campaign activities. They note that John Hay, a Republican, accused Bryan of "begging for the presidency as a tramp might beg for a pie." But while McKinley won from his front porch against the barnstorming Bryan, presidential candidates who came after acted much more like Bryan than McKinley. Outright electioneering, once a tactic many thought beneath presidential candidates—perhaps born out of the Washingtonian idea that the office seeks the man, as opposed to the other way around—would become both common and something that voters would expect of candidates.[19]

While the completeness of Nixon's campaign strategy in 1960 was novel, the general concept—hit as many states as possible—was not. And there were good reasons for candidates to approach presidential elections as national affairs—the best one being that they were just that. Nixon knew that he could not plausibly compete in all 50 states in 1960, but many were extremely close—20 states were decided by less than five percentage points. The same was true in 1976, when Carter defeated Ford by two points nationally (Kennedy won the national vote by less than two-tenths of a point against Nixon).

It stands to reason that there would be a lot of close states in a close election, although that has become less true over time. For instance, in Republican George W. Bush's victory in 2000 over Democrat Al Gore, 12 states were decided by less than five points. Four years later, in Bush's 2.5-point national win over Democrat John Kerry, 11 state margins were less than five points. By 2012, just four states were decided by less than five points in Democrat Barack Obama's four-point national win over Republican Mitt Romney: Florida, North Carolina, Ohio, and Virginia. So while those elections were slightly more (2000) or slightly less (2004, 2012) competitive than those of 1960 and 1976, the more recent contests featured fewer true swing states.

But that doesn't tell the whole story, because 1960, 1976, 2000, 2004, and 2012 were all nationally competitive elections. There's a way to measure how many states vote close to the national average in both close elections and blowouts.

## The Two-Party Vote and Presidential Deviation

There are two concepts that merit explaining before proceeding. The first is the two-party vote.

This is simple enough. The two-party vote is a way of reporting election results as just the votes cast for the Democratic and Republican candidates in a given race. It subtracts the third-party votes, allowing for comparisons across time without the distorting effects independent and minor party candidacies have on results. Given the longstanding dominance of the two parties, this is a way to cut out the noise that fleeting third-party insurgencies introduce from time to time.

In most modern elections, removing the third-party vote barely makes a difference at all. For instance, in 2004, 2008, and 2012, 99 percent, 98 percent, and 98 percent of all the presidential votes cast, respectively, were for the Democratic and Republican candidates. Removing the third-party votes hardly alters the margins of victory at all. In 2012, Obama beat Romney by 3.86 percentage points in the all-party voting, versus 3.92 points in the two-party vote. In other words, there was no real difference.

However, using the two-party vote creates complications for certain years featuring big third-party votes, like 1912, 1924, 1968, 1992, and 1996, among other years. But only Democratic and Republican candidates have won the presidency since both parties began competing against each other in 1856. Third-party candidates occasionally win electoral votes, but only rarely: the last one to win any state was race-baiting George Wallace in 1968, who won five southern states as an independent candidate.

The main reason to use the two-party vote is to make apples-to-apples comparisons over time. Using two back-to-back elections from the 2000s illustrates why this can be a useful exercise.

In 2000, Gore received 48.4 percent of the total national vote (including all votes cast for all candidates). Four years later, Kerry got 48.3 percent of the all-party total vote. By that metric, it appears that Gore and Kerry performed almost exactly the same.

But in practice, Gore did significantly better, winning the popular vote by about half a percentage point while Kerry lost by about 2.5 points in the national popular vote to Bush. The difference between those years is that close to 4 percent of all voters in 2000 voted for third-party candidates—mostly for Green Party nominee Ralph Nader, who probably cost Gore the election—while just 1 percent of all voters picked a third-party candidate in 2004. The national two-party vote in those years tells the more accurate tale. Gore won 50.3 percent of the two-party tally in 2000, while Kerry captured just 48.8 percent four years later.

Third-party candidacies come and go, but since 1856 the two major parties have remained constant, and tracking the change in the votes for these parties paints a clearer picture about the evolution of the nation's voting from election to election. While there will be exceptions, most of the results reported throughout the rest of the book will be just the two-party vote.

The second concept is presidential deviation. This is the difference between how a county, state, or other political subdivision votes in a given election compared with, usually, the national results. It's a way of expressing how reflective a given place is of the national results. This is, again, calculated through the two-party vote (although it can be figured through the all-party vote just as well) and it's expressed as a rounded number.[20]

For instance, the national two-party vote in 2012 was 52 percent to 48 percent in favor of Obama over Romney. That same year, Romney won Wyoming 71 percent to 29 percent. Romney's share of the vote in Wyoming was 23 percentage points larger than his national share (and Obama's was 23 points lower—again, all numbers are rounded). So Wyoming deviated 23 points from the national average in 2012 in favor of the Republicans. For shorthand, this makes Wyoming an R +23 state.

Measuring this deviation isolates where a state stands in relation to the national voting in elections that are both narrow and lopsided. For instance, in Virginia in 1976, Ford beat Carter by about two points. Four years later, Virginia backed Reagan by about 14 points. That's a 12-point swing in the two-party vote. But its presidential deviation from the nation was the same in both elections: it was two points more Republican than the nation in 1976 (narrowly backing Ford while Carter won nationally) and then two points more Republican in 1980 (giving Reagan a slightly bigger victory than in his overall national triumph). So, while Virginia's margin of victory for the Republican presidential candidate changed quite a bit from 1976 to 1980, the Old Dominion didn't get any more Republican relative to the nation from one year to the next. The deviation separates the swing in the state from the swing nationally.

Presidential deviation is used later in this book to compare county-level results to state and national results, placing the outcome in certain places in both state-level and national-level contexts. For instance, in Ohio in 2008, Obama got 52 percent of the two-party vote, while he got 54 percent nationally. In Athens County, home of Ohio University, he got 68 percent of the vote. So Athens County was D +16 compared to the state versus D +14 compared to the nation.

### THE NATION'S SHRINKING MIDDLE

The two-party vote metric, combined with presidential deviation, makes it possible to compare election results over time. It also illustrates which states were close to the national presidential voting average in both blow-outs and nail-biters.

The 1960 election, when 20 states were decided by five points or less in the all-party vote, is already noted above. Compare that to 1956, Eisenhower's reelection victory. That year, only three states were decided by less than five points.

But the two elections are not really comparable: Ike captured 457 electoral votes and 57 percent of the national popular vote against Stevenson in their rematch from four years prior. One wouldn't expect there to be many close states in such a lopsided election—but looking at the election through presidential deviation tells a far different tale.

A whopping 32 states had deviations of less than five points in 1956, one more than the much closer 1960 election. (Less than five points means any state with a deviation of four or less in the election. Practically speaking, because of rounding, this means any state with a deviation of less than 4.5 points.) This can be less than five points in either direction, which is actually a fairly large range: In an election that was 50–50 nationally, a state that voted 54 percent to 46 percent either way would be included in this definition as a state with a deviation less than five.

The examples of 1956 and 1960 represent a high-water mark for the number of states clustered near the nation's middle in the 30 presidential elections from 1896 to 2012. They also represent a high mark for the number of *electoral votes* in states with deviations of four or less. In those two elections, roughly three-quarters of all the available electoral votes were in the states with low deviations. Those are also the two highest in the time frame studied.

So an equal number of states were clustered close to the national average in both elections—it's just that Eisenhower's much higher tide of victory meant that the states voting with the middle of the country were giving Ike big victories that mirrored his national victory, while JFK's tiny tide meant that those states whose voting deviated only narrowly from the national voting mimicked Kennedy's narrow 50-state win, and thus were close in absolute terms as well.

Figure 1.1 shows the number of electoral votes in states that voted close to the national popular vote in a given election from 1896 through 2012. As should be clear from figure 1.1, the number of electoral votes in states that vote near the national average has been dropping over the last several decades.

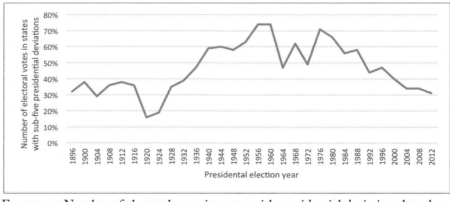

FIGURE 1.1. Number of electoral votes in states with presidential deviations less than five in presidential elections, 1896–2012

The figure shows how the number of states—and the number of electoral votes—that reside near the nation's political middle was about as low in the mid-2010s as it was a century earlier. The number dipped to very low levels in the first part of the 20th century. They steadily rose throughout the dozen years of Democrat Franklin D. Roosevelt's presidency, staying generally high through the very close election of 1976, before steadily declining over the past four decades.

That suggests a sorting of the states into opposing camps with near-impregnable walls, making most states effectively uncompetitive in tight national elections. This dovetails with other trends in American politics and culture.

## SORTED AMERICA

Bill Bishop argued in *The Big Sort* that the United States is becoming increasingly clustered, with like-minded people choosing to live closer together. This sorting, Bishop argues, is reflected in our politics: "As people seek out the social settings they prefer—as they choose the group that makes them feel the most comfortable—the nation grows more politically segregated—and the benefit that ought to come with having a variety of opinions is lost to the righteousness that is the special entitlement of homogenous groups."[21]

A yawning urban/rural split has emerged in the nation's politics, with Democrats performing well in big urban counties while Republicans win much of what remains. In 2012, Obama captured 46 of the nation's 50 most populous counties. Back in 1976, Carter won just 27 of these counties against Ford.

Obama won only 7 percent of counties that are part of Appalachia, the country's sparsely populated and historically economically depressed region that is defined by the federal Appalachian Regional Commission.[22] In his 1976 victory, Carter won about 70 percent of these counties; in 1996, Democratic incumbent Bill Clinton won nearly half of them. Both of these candidates, as southerners, had special appeal to this culturally southern-leaning region, but the disparity in performance in such a short amount of time remains striking.

In the 2012 election, roughly four-fifths of nonwhite voters, who made up close to 30 percent of the national electorate, voted for Obama, while about three-fifths of white voters, making up about 70 percent of the voters, picked Romney.[23] As the country becomes more diverse, it's not impossible to imagine a scenario where voting becomes even more polarized by race.

Others have noted the increasing political polarization of the American public, such as Alan Abramowitz, who coined along with his colleague Steven Webster the term "negative partisanship," which describes how voters' increasingly hostile perceptions of the opposing political party inform their voting. "This has led to sharp increases in party loyalty and straight ticket voting across all categories of party identification," they write, "and to growing consistency between the results of presidential elections and the results of House and Senate elections."[24]

In 1900, just 3.4 percent of US House districts featured split results— that is, only a relative handful of districts supported a different party for president and for US representative. Such low percentages remained common throughout the first half of the 20th century: on average, only 12 percent of districts featured split results in the presidential elections held during this period. (Not all district results are available from this time period, but there's little reason to think that the missing data would change the results much.)

But throughout the second half of the century and into this century, it was common for congressional districts to support candidates from different parties for president and for the US House. From 1952 to 2008, an average of 28 percent of House districts split their presidential and congressional ballots. However, the number of split districts has been dropping over time, bottoming out at only 26 of 435 districts (6 percent) in 2012.[25]

Granted, blowout elections will naturally produce more split districts. The two elections with the highest number of split district results were 1972 and 1984, when Republicans Richard Nixon and Ronald Reagan each carried 49 of 50 states in smashing reelections. Also, both parties will draw favorable districts for themselves whenever possible, a process known as gerrymandering. This incentivizes the majority party in a state to draw the minority party's voters into a small number of districts the majority party cannot win, while drawing a larger number of safe districts for themselves.

But the trend over time is a good measure of polarization—and also of the political trajectory of the South, which throughout the second half of the 20th century often elected Democrats to the House while backing Republicans for president. Indeed, the less polarized second half of the last decade doesn't exactly have noble roots. Brendan Nyhan has argued that "the less polarized politics of the mid-20th century were driven almost entirely by the issue of race, which created a bloc of conservative southern Democrats who acted as a virtual third party for much of this time."[26]

Those conservative Democrats in the South would become Republicans: the Deep South (Alabama, Georgia, Mississippi, Louisiana, and South Carolina) is now largely a one-party preserve. The same can be said of several other southern states, such as Arkansas, Tennessee, and Texas.

The Republican Party used to have a bloc of northeastern liberals/moderates, known as "Rockefeller Republicans" in tribute to the moderate governor of New York, Nelson Rockefeller. One of the last examples of these political anachronisms was Senator Lincoln Chafee of Rhode Island, who lost to a Democrat in the midterm wave of 2006. Nearly a decade later, in 2015, Chafee was not only a Democrat—he was running (hopelessly) for the Democratic presidential nomination before dropping out of the race after a single debate.

The reason to bring all this up is simple: in a divided political world where so few voters and states can be reached, the few states that are near the nation's political center become even more valuable. When many states are near the average national voting—as was the case in 1960 and 1976, for instance—a truly national electoral strategy is sensible. But when few are, as has been the case in recent elections, much of the country can and should be ignored by any sane presidential campaign.

## THE NARROW ELECTORAL BATTLEFIELD

Nowadays, a Nixonian 50-state pledge would be ridiculous. According to an analysis from the Center for Voting and Democracy, the 2012 presidential candidates—President Obama and running mate Joe Biden along with Mitt Romney and running mate Paul Ryan—held public events in only 12 states after the Democratic National Convention, all of which would deviate less than five points from the national average.[27] Both parties had an excellent grasp of what the closest states were. If anything, noting that the candidates visited a dozen states makes the number of truly competitive states seem artificially high: the listing includes only one visit apiece in Michigan and Minnesota, and five or fewer in North Carolina and Pennsylvania. The remaining eight states enjoyed—endured?—243 visits from the presidential tickets. Nearly a third of those were in Ohio, whose 73 visits were more than double the total of any other state except for Florida, which had 40.

Additionally, the Center found that the two campaigns spent more than 99 percent of their respective television campaign advertising dollars in just 10 states from mid-April (when Romney effectively clinched the GOP nomination) through the November general election: Colorado, Florida, Iowa, Nevada, New Hampshire, North Carolina, Pennsylvania, Ohio, Virginia, and Wisconsin. Few would be surprised if these 10 states again ate up nearly all the resources spent by the two major-party nominees in the 2016 presidential election.

If campaigns were run 100 years ago the way they are today, with the same technology, extensive candidate travel, and micro-targeting of television ads, a similar dynamic would have prevailed. A small number of electoral votes—36 percent of them in 1916 in 21 states, versus 31 percent of them in 14 states in 2012—would have been in play (with eventual presidential deviations less than five points), and the campaigns in both eras would have been wise to focus only on these states.

The difference would have been in the states targeted. Only five of them appear on both 1916's list of states closest to the national average and 2012's: Minnesota, New Hampshire, New Mexico, Oregon, and Ohio. In both eras, Ohio was by far the most valuable prize among these states: in 1916, it had double (24) the number of electoral votes of its next closest rival among this group, Minnesota (12), and in 2012 it had nearly double the electoral votes (18) of the second-ranked state among this group, again Minnesota (10). Additionally, while Minnesota, New Mexico, and

Oregon are included here as competitive, they really weren't in 2012: New Mexico and Oregon did not see a single dollar of ad spending and neither presidential ticket visited them, while Minnesota saw only a pittance of ad spending and a single visit, by Ryan.

Ohio spent the entire post–Civil War era—and, really, before that as well—voting at or near the national political midpoint. Sometimes it had a lot of company in this position, particularly in the middle of the 20th century. Other times—including the elections in the 21st century held while many states were moving further toward the Democrats or the Republicans—it was one of relatively few prizes plausibly available to both parties in a competitive national election. In fact, there's a lot of evidence that suggests that Ohio has been the best bellwether state in presidential elections for a century or more.

# Two

## Ohio at the Head of the Flock

In the late stages of the 2012 presidential campaign, a disconnect emerged between national horse-race polls for the presidential race and those at the state level. Republican Mitt Romney thoroughly outperformed Democratic incumbent Barack Obama in the first presidential debate, held about a month before Election Day, and surged in national polls. Romney took a small lead immediately after the debate and then held within one point of Obama in averages of national polls for the remainder of the campaign, according to the widely cited RealClearPolitics website's average of national polls.[1] The Gallup daily presidential tracker, posted promptly at 1:00 p.m. Eastern Time every day and immediately dissected by political journalists and junkies, proved particularly favorable for Romney, showing him with leads in the mid-single digits for much of the rest of the campaign before narrowing to a final prediction of Romney 49 percent, Obama 48 percent.[2]

Yet, while the national polls were showing a race that was effectively a tie, the state-level polls in one key state were telling a different story. In Ohio, Obama consistently led Romney for the entirety of the race in nearly every poll, including those conducted at the high-water mark for Romney after the first debate. Of 85 polls conducted in the state during the 2012 calendar year, just nine ever showed Romney leading. Eight showed ties, and Obama led the rest.[3]

The incumbent's lead in the state proved durable, and the polls almost exactly nailed his victory margin. The final RealClearPolitics average showed Obama with a lead of 2.9 percentage points, and he would win the state by three points. The accurate Ohio polling was an exception in 2012, though: Obama led on Election Day in the RealClearPolitics average of national polls by less than a point while winning nationally by four, and the averaged polls of many of the other swing states generally undershot Obama's final margin by roughly three to four points. There was no way to know before the election with certainty that Ohio's polls would be correct and so many of the national and other state polls would be off. But in hindsight they were a strong sign Obama would win not just Ohio, but nationally as well. Overall, the winning presidential candidate has carried Ohio in 28 of the last 30 elections, so the Ohio polling suggested an Obama win.

While Obama could have won the White House without Ohio, the president's victory kept alive a dubious streak for Republicans: they still have never won a presidential election without Ohio, going back to the party's first presidential election in 1856, when Republican John C. Frémont captured the state but lost the election to Democrat James Buchanan.

Not only has no Republican ever won the White House without carrying Ohio, but the state is typically more Republican than the nation as a whole. In the last 30 elections, the Democratic presidential candidate has outperformed his national average in Ohio only six times. This alone should have suggested that either the national polls showing what was basically a tied race, or the Ohio polls indicating a small lead for Obama, were wrong in 2012: it would be historically out of step for a Democrat to significantly outperform his national performance in the Buckeye State.

So the Ohio polling suggested not just an Obama win, but a national victory of more than three points—but not by much more than three points. Ohio's two-party presidential vote has not deviated more than three points from the national average in any election since the conclusion of World War II. Thus, the Ohio polling would have suggested an Obama win of more than three points but less than six points. Obama won by four.

The long historical record suggests that, with just a few exceptions, Ohio has long mimicked the national voting, and that it has done so better than any other state. The case for Ohio as the nation's top bellwether state is therefore threefold:

1. Ohio has the best record of any state in voting for the winning candidate.

2. Ohio's results most often reflect the national voting average.

3. Ohio has provided the decisive electoral votes to the winning candidate more times than any other state.

WINS AND LOSSES

This book focuses on the presidential elections from 1896 through 2012. Why begin there?

The 1896 election began a 30-cycle span, running through 2012, during which Ohio voted for the winning presidential candidate in all but two elections: 1944 and 1960. By percentage, that's the best record for any state over those 116 years. While Ohio's voting consistently came close to the national average prior to 1896, a logical place to begin this study is at the beginning of its long and rarely broken streak of voting for presidential winners.

Beyond that, historical and ideological reasons urge starting in 1896. Political scientists have long regarded 1896 as a seminal, realigning election.[4] It ended a post-Reconstruction electoral era, from 1876 to 1892, of extremely close presidential elections that featured not one, but two, Electoral College "misfires," where the winner of the national popular vote lost the presidency (Democrats Samuel Tilden in 1876 and incumbent President Grover Cleveland in 1888). Ohio Republican William McKinley's more than four-point margin in 1896 was the biggest victory since Republican Ulysses S. Grant's 12-point reelection triumph in 1872.

More important, 1896 represented an ideological shift in one of the parties. Democratic nominee William Jennings Bryan pushed for the free coinage of silver, co-opting the agrarian Populist movement that had supported James Weaver's third-party candidacy in 1892, when Weaver received close to 9 percent of the vote and carried five states. Bryan's silver stance alienated the Democrats' business wing. The sitting Democratic president, Cleveland, had little use for Bryan, and many Cleveland Democrats deserted the party (including the president, who supported McKinley).

The Democratic Party changed in 1896, even if the voter coalition that supported Bryan looked a lot like the old Democratic coalition (the party's base would change over time). The political scientist John Gerring, in his study of party ideology in American presidential politics, characterizes the pre-1896 Democrats as a party aligned with the principles of Founding Father Thomas Jefferson, such as promoting "liberty versus tyranny" and opposing the growth of the state. The post-1896 Democrats are a populist party, he argued, concerned with "the people versus the interests." The Republican Party's ideological shift from a nationalist party of promoting "order versus anarchy" to a party defined by "the state versus the individual" came later, in the 1920s, likely as a result of Democratic President Woodrow Wilson's growing of government during his term (cemented by Democratic President Franklin Roosevelt's liberalism during his more than a decade in office).[5] In effect, Bryan—who was also the Populist Party nominee—brought the populists into the Democratic Party, but the Democrats lost more than they gained and remained in the presidential wilderness for 16 years, until a Republican Party split allowed the Democrats to win the presidency in 1912 (and then hold it against a unified GOP in 1916).

There's something symbolic, too, about 1896 from an Ohio perspective. The country in 1896 came to where Ohio already was. Since the founding of the Republican Party in the early 1850s—the party first produced a presidential candidate, Frémont, in 1856—the GOP carried Ohio in every election through 1896.

That coincided with a golden age for Ohio in national politics. McKinley's victory in 1896 marked the sixth time in eight elections that a native Ohioan was elected to the White House—Grant twice (in 1868 and 1872), Rutherford B. Hayes (1876), James A. Garfield (1880), Benjamin Harrison (1888), and McKinley. Four years later, McKinley would make it seven Ohio victories in nine tries, before he, like Garfield before him, fell victim to an assassin's bullet shortly after the beginning of his second term.

Ohio would vote Republican in every election from 1856 to 1912, and so would the nation, save for just two elections: Cleveland's victories in 1884 and 1892. Into the 1910s and throughout the rest of the 20th century into the 21st, the nation would swing back and forth between the parties, with Ohio almost always close to the national average. More narrowly, given that McKinley was an Ohioan—as was his political Svengali, Mark Hanna—that's also a reason to start with 1896 here.

Table 2.1 shows how many times each state voted for the presidential winner over the 30 elections from 1896 through 2012.[6] Some of the states did not exist in 1896, so their record of voting with winners begins in the first election in which they participated. For instance, New Mexico became a state in time for the 1912 election, so it voted in 26 elections over this time frame instead of 30, like Ohio.

#### Table 2.1. Electoral record of the states over the last 30 elections, 1896–2012

| State | Total wins | Total elections | Percentage | State | Total wins | Total elections | Percentage |
|---|---|---|---|---|---|---|---|
| Ohio | 28 | 30 | 93% | Minnesota | 22 | 30 | 73% |
| New Mexico | 24 | 26 | 92% | Tennessee | 22 | 30 | 73% |
| Illinois | 26 | 30 | 87% | Utah | 22 | 30 | 73% |
| Nevada | 26 | 30 | 87% | Washington | 22 | 30 | 73% |
| California | 25 | 30 | 83% | Wyoming | 22 | 30 | 73% |
| Delaware | 25 | 30 | 83% | Oklahoma | 19 | 27 | 70% |
| Maryland | 25 | 30 | 83% | North Dakota | 21 | 30 | 70% |
| Missouri | 25 | 30 | 83% | Indiana | 21 | 30 | 70% |
| New Hampshire | 25 | 30 | 83% | Kansas | 20 | 30 | 67% |
| New Jersey | 25 | 30 | 83% | Virginia | 20 | 30 | 67% |
| New York | 24 | 30 | 80% | Hawaii | 9 | 14 | 64% |
| Arizona | 20 | 26 | 77% | Maine | 19 | 30 | 63% |
| Connecticut | 23 | 30 | 77% | Nebraska | 19 | 30 | 63% |
| Iowa | 23 | 30 | 77% | North Carolina | 19 | 30 | 63% |
| Massachusetts | 23 | 30 | 77% | Texas | 19 | 30 | 63% |
| Montana | 23 | 30 | 77% | Vermont | 19 | 30 | 63% |
| Oregon | 23 | 30 | 77% | Arkansas | 18 | 30 | 60% |
| Pennsylvania | 23 | 30 | 77% | South Dakota | 18 | 30 | 60% |
| Rhode Island | 23 | 30 | 77% | Alaska | 8 | 14 | 57% |
| West Virginia | 23 | 30 | 77% | Louisiana | 17 | 30 | 57% |
| Wisconsin | 23 | 30 | 77% | Georgia | 15 | 30 | 50% |
| Colorado | 22 | 30 | 73% | South Carolina | 15 | 30 | 50% |
| Florida | 22 | 30 | 73% | Alabama | 14 | 30 | 47% |
| Idaho | 22 | 30 | 73% | District of Columbia | 6 | 13 | 46% |
| Kentucky | 22 | 30 | 73% | Mississippi | 13 | 30 | 43% |
| Michigan | 22 | 30 | 73% | | | | |

The most Democratic region in the first half of this 30-election time frame was the South, which voted almost uniformly Democratic from Reconstruction through the presidency of Franklin Roosevelt. A confluence of factors, including the Democratic Party's increasing policy liberalism, its post–World War II embrace of civil rights activism on behalf of blacks (who began to vote heavily Democratic during Roosevelt's term in response to the New Deal), and increasing migration of northern Republicans to growing southern cities like Charlotte, Atlanta, and others, pushed the historically conservative South to align itself with what was becoming the clearly more conservative party, the Republicans.[7]

But, for the first half of this period, the South voted Democratic almost all the time, and given that the Republicans won the White House in seven of nine elections from 1896 to 1928, many of the southern states racked up a lot of presidential campaign losses by voting for Democrats. By the 2010s, Republicans dominated eight of the 11 states of the old Confederacy—Alabama, Arkansas, Georgia, Louisiana, Mississippi, South Carolina, Tennessee, and Texas—and thus they all comfortably supported Republicans John McCain in 2008 and Mitt Romney in 2012 while the nation was voting for Barack Obama.

Meanwhile, the remaining three ex-Confederate states—Florida, North Carolina, and Virginia—all eventually became swing states, with Virginia moving from rock-solid Republicanism in presidential elections (it was the only southern state to vote against evangelical Christian Democrat Jimmy Carter in 1976) to the nation's political center, closely mirroring the national vote in both 2008 and 2012.

Florida and North Carolina retain slight GOP leans but are battleground states (the Sunshine State) or are trending in that direction (the Tar Heel State). In any event, bloc voting first for Democrats and then for Republicans in the South makes it hard to argue that any of these states are historic bellwethers, even though demographic changes might make those latter three states along the Atlantic Coast among the most reliable bellwethers going forward, perhaps surpassing even a state like Ohio.

In the Northeast, the poor records of Maine and Vermont stand out, primarily because they are the only two states to never vote for FDR, fighting off the eventual four-term president's advances even in his landslide reelection triumph of 1936.

New England Republicanism, like the South's Democratic tradition, was a feature of a political system where presidential elections were effectively reruns of the Civil War held every four years, with the North Republican, the South Democratic, and the battlegrounds of the Midwest and Border States oscillating in competitive years. Modern party labels tell us little about the ideology of the time. Just because Maine and Vermont never voted for Roosevelt, while Alabama and Mississippi provided him with such towering totals that the results seem to resemble sham elections held in dictatorships, didn't necessarily make the former pair "conservative" and the latter pair "liberal" by the 21st-century definitions of the terms.

There's a saying that "As goes Maine, so goes the nation." That wasn't because it was a bellwether; as shown above, Maine was a reliably Republican state in presidential elections for much of its history. The saying comes from the fact that until 1958 the state voted in September as opposed to November for nonpresidential offices, which most states adopted as a national election date following the Civil War. RealClearPolitics analyst Sean Trende noted in 2010 that "this enabled prognosticators to get a good sense of which way the winds were blowing. If Republicans did well, they could expect a decent year nationally. If the races were close, it was probably not going to be a good year. And if Democrats actually won a few races, Republicans knew to run for cover nationwide."[8] In 1936, Maine's early vote backed the GOP in multiple statewide offices and the Pine Tree State's three US House districts, suggesting a Republican turn nationally. Instead, FDR won a smashing reelection, losing only two states (Maine and Vermont, noted above). That led to a revision: "As goes Maine, so goes Vermont."[9]

Massachusetts and Rhode Island have better records in part because they turned reliably Democratic much earlier than some of their New England neighbors. Both states voted for Catholic Democrat Al Smith, the governor of New York, in 1928. While Smith was soundly defeated by Republican Herbert Hoover—losing even some states in the South, thanks in part to his religion and his urban politics—his nomination excited his coreligionists and immigrants in big cities, stirring a new base that Roosevelt would bring solidly into the Democratic Party during his presidency.

OHIO'S MIDWESTERN COMPETITION

The Midwest features three states that election watchers have cited at various times as bellwethers: Illinois, Missouri, and Ohio. But while the bellwether label has fit at certain points, developments in Illinois and Missouri, and also nationally, made both these states less reliable presidential predictors in the 21st century.

A growing political separation between urban and rural America—cities becoming ever more Democratic while rural areas have become increasingly Republican—has tilted Illinois strongly to the Democrats thanks to the increasingly Democratic lean of Cook County, home of Chicago, the Midwest's biggest city.

Illinois gave up its bellwether status by voting comfortably for Al Gore in 2000 and John Kerry in 2004, and no one expected it to go Republican in 2016 unless the GOP ran up a national margin of Ronald Reagan-esque proportions. It just isn't really winnable for Republicans anymore in a close national election.

In the midst of the 2004 presidential campaign, the *Economist* declared, not inaccurately at the time, that "Missouri has an almost mythical reputation in American presidential politics."[10] The state had voted for the presidential victor in every election but one since 1904, and it was poised once again to play an outsized role in another close race. Indeed, Missouri ended up voting with the winner—Republican George W. Bush—but Bush did about two and a half points better in the Show-Me State than he did nationally, while Democrat John Kerry did about two points worse. It was the third election in a row that Missouri had voted slightly more Republican than the nation, a tiny lean that would become more pronounced.

Missouri has of late tilted away from the Midwest and toward the South, and there are not enough Democratic votes in the state's two major cities, St. Louis and Kansas City, to make up for the rest of the state becoming reliably Republican.[11] After fulfilling its bellwether role for the 25th time in 26 elections in 2004, Missouri resisted the country's clear Democratic swing to Obama in 2008, voting narrowly for John McCain. By 2012, Missouri voted seven points more Republican than the nation as a whole—the GOP's best performance in the state relative to the national results since the Civil War. Missouri often leaned toward its southern neighbors throughout its history, including in 1956, when it was the only non-Confederate state to back Democrat Adlai Stevenson against Republican President Dwight Eisenhower.

Only 10 states voted for both parties at least once in the four elections from 2000 to 2012. Illinois and Missouri were not among them; one uniformly backed the Democrats (the Land of Lincoln), the other, Republicans (the Show-Me State). Ohio, meanwhile, voted with the winner in all four elections and mirrored the national vote in each election.

## The Western Bellwethers

Out west, California, Nevada, and New Mexico have strong histories of voting for presidential winners, although there is increasing evidence that two of the three—the Golden State and the Land of Enchantment—are, like Illinois, moving more reliably into the Democratic column.

Shocking as it may seem to those familiar with only 21st-century results, California went Republican in all but one election—the Lyndon Johnson 1964 landslide—from 1952 through 1988. However, a Californian was on the Republican ticket in all but three of those 10 elections: Richard Nixon was Dwight Eisenhower's running mate in 1952 and 1956, and the GOP nominee in his own right in 1960, 1968, and 1972, while former California Governor Ronald Reagan was the Republican nominee in 1980 and 1984. Throughout this period, California was not noticeably more Republican than the nation as a whole, and its failure to vote for Carter in the very close 1976 election was part of a broader problem for the Democrat that year: he proved to have very little appeal west of the Mississippi River (the farthest west state he carried was Texas, which has voted more often with the South than the West throughout its history). No one would have called California a bellwether in the 2010s, given how reliably Democratic it became, thanks to the dominance of its big, urban centers along the coast and growing population of Democratic-leaning nonwhite voters.

If one just went back over the last hundred years of elections (it didn't become a state until 1912), New Mexico would match Ohio as having the best record in voting with the winning presidential candidate. But the Land of Enchantment—where about two in five voters were Hispanic in 2012[12]—might also be shifting more reliably into the Democratic column. It was more Democratic in 2008 and 2012 than it had been since Harry Truman's victory in 1948. Both presidential campaigns largely ignored the state in 2012, and Obama won it by 10 points.

With its historically large Hispanic population, New Mexico doesn't look much like the nation. John Petrocik commenting in 1996 on New Mexico's history of backing winners in presidential elections, noted, "The problem is that New Mexico doesn't look like anyplace else. It's too atypical and out of the way for people to take its bellwether status as anything but luck or accident, even though that might not be the case."[13] If Hispanics continue to vote for Democrats at a rate of two-thirds or better—a big if, because such voting patterns are not necessarily set in stone—New Mexico may move to the Democrats as Missouri has shifted toward the Republicans.

Nevada is a different story. From 1912 to 2012, Nevada voted against the winner just once, when it narrowly supported unelected incumbent Ford over Carter in 1976. Its modern bellwether role can be attributed to being "representative of America," according to Nevada political reporter and analyst Jon Ralston.

> Urban and rural, growing Hispanic population, a fast-growing melting pot until the recession slowed us down. Nevada really is three states, which put together form a whole that would reflect the nation's sentiments. Super-urban Clark County, with the biggest city and all the concomitant problems, issues of a big city, and heavily Democratic; urban Reno, a small-town feel, the swing county that has liberals more liberal than Clark and conservatives more conservative; the other 15 counties, all rural, very conservative, a picture of red America. . . . Why wouldn't we be representative?[14]

Demographically, Nevada provides what could be a vision of the nation's future. According to the 2012 general election exit poll (a survey taken of voters at polling places after they voted), Nevada's voters were eight points more diverse than the nation's: 64 percent White (compared to 72 percent nationally), 19 percent Hispanic/Latino, 9 percent Black, 5 percent Asian American, 4 percent Other.[15]

All in all, there's a good argument for Nevada as a premier bellwether going forward. But there's more to determining a bellwether than just whether a state votes with the winners.

### OHIO: ALWAYS IN THE MIDDLE

Another way to measure how much a state's results reflect the national average is looking at how far the state deviates from the national results. For this, let's return to the presidential deviations explained in the first chapter. As a refresher, the presidential deviation shows how far away from the national vote a state's results were in a given year, using just the two-party vote. In a 50–50 national election, a state that voted 55 percent to 45 percent for the Democrat would be D +5, and a state that voted 55 percent to 45 percent for the Republican would be R +5. The bigger the deviation, the further a state's results are from the national popular vote.

Table 2.2 shows how many times from 1896 through 2012 each state had a presidential deviation that was less than five. States that are generally close to the national voting can be considered bellwethers; states that are not are outliers.

### Table 2.2. States with presidential deviations less than five in presidential elections, 1896–2012

| State | No. of times with sub-five presidential deviations | Total elections 1896–2012 | Percentage | State | No. of times with sub-five presidential deviations | Total elections 1896–2012 | Percentage |
|---|---|---|---|---|---|---|---|
| Ohio | 27 | 30 | 90% | Hawaii | 5 | 14 | 36% |
| New Mexico | 20 | 26 | 77% | Idaho | 9 | 30 | 30% |
| Delaware | 20 | 30 | 67% | Maine | 9 | 30 | 30% |
| Illinois | 20 | 30 | 67% | Arizona | 7 | 26 | 27% |
| Missouri | 20 | 30 | 67% | Kansas | 8 | 30 | 27% |
| Oregon | 20 | 30 | 67% | Louisiana | 8 | 30 | 27% |
| Kentucky | 19 | 30 | 63% | North Carolina | 8 | 30 | 27% |
| Maryland | 19 | 30 | 63% | North Dakota | 8 | 30 | 27% |
| Montana | 19 | 30 | 63% | Texas | 8 | 30 | 27% |
| Pennsylvania | 19 | 30 | 63% | Wyoming | 8 | 30 | 27% |
| Michigan | 18 | 30 | 60% | Massachusetts | 7 | 30 | 23% |
| New Jersey | 18 | 30 | 60% | Rhode Island | 7 | 30 | 23% |
| Nevada | 18 | 30 | 60% | South Dakota | 7 | 30 | 23% |
| Washington | 18 | 30 | 60% | Tennessee | 7 | 30 | 23% |
| West Virginia | 18 | 30 | 60% | Oklahoma | 6 | 27 | 22% |
| California | 17 | 30 | 57% | Alaska | 3 | 14 | 21% |
| Iowa | 17 | 30 | 57% | Arkansas | 6 | 30 | 20% |
| New Hampshire | 17 | 30 | 57% | Utah | 6 | 30 | 20% |
| Connecticut | 16 | 30 | 53% | Nebraska | 5 | 30 | 17% |
| Minnesota | 16 | 30 | 53% | Vermont | 5 | 30 | 17% |
| New York | 16 | 30 | 53% | Georgia | 3 | 30 | 10% |
| Wisconsin | 15 | 30 | 50% | Mississippi | 2 | 30 | 7% |
| Indiana | 14 | 30 | 47% | Alabama | 1 | 30 | 3% |
| Colorado | 14 | 30 | 47% | South Carolina | 1 | 30 | 3% |
| Florida | 11 | 30 | 37% | Dist. of Columbia | 0 | 13 | 0% |
| Virginia | 11 | 30 | 37% | | | | |

Amazingly, Ohio's presidential deviation has been five points or more only three times in the last 30 elections, by far the lowest of any states. New Mexico comes in second, at six of the last 26 (it first voted for president in 1912). Other than those two states, no other has been near the national average in more than 75 percent of the presidential elections over this 116-year time period. In fact, 29 of the 51 states (including the District of Columbia) have more often than not had presidential results that have been significantly outside the national mainstream.

The District of Columbia, with its heavy Democratic lean, has *never* been within five points of the national voting (it first voted for president in 1964). The formerly Democratic Solid South, which is now staunchly Republican, is almost a perfect anti-bellwether: Alabama and South Carolina have had deviations less than five points in only two of the last 30 elections, and Mississippi only did twice.

Table 2.3 shows the average presidential deviation for each state over the past 30 elections. For each election, it doesn't matter whether a state deviated in a Democratic or a Republican direction—the average deviation in either direction over the 30 elections is what's expressed here.

### Table 2.3. States' average deviation from two-party presidential vote, 1896–2012

| State | Average deviation from national vote | State | Average deviation from national vote | State | Average deviation from national vote |
|---|---|---|---|---|---|
| Ohio | 2.2 | Colorado | 5.2 | Rhode Island | 8.9 |
| New Mexico | 2.8 | Michigan | 5.3 | North Carolina | 9.0 |
| Illinois | 3.6 | Montana | 5.4 | North Dakota | 9.2 |
| Missouri | 3.7 | New Hampshire | 5.4 | Alaska | 9.3 |
| Delaware | 3.7 | Nevada | 5.5 | Nebraska | 9.5 |
| Oregon | 3.8 | California | 5.7 | Idaho | 10.1 |
| New Jersey | 3.9 | Minnesota | 5.9 | Utah | 11.4 |
| Iowa | 4.2 | Tennessee | 7.0 | Florida | 12.4 |
| Maryland | 4.4 | Arizona | 7.3 | Vermont | 12.5 |
| Pennsylvania | 4.5 | Maine | 7.5 | Arkansas | 13.4 |
| Indiana | 4.5 | Kansas | 8.0 | Texas | 15.1 |
| Connecticut | 4.7 | Hawaii | 8.2 | Georgia | 18.7 |
| West Virginia | 4.7 | Virginia | 8.3 | Louisiana | 18.8 |
| Kentucky | 4.9 | South Dakota | 8.5 | Alabama | 20.1 |
| New York | 5.0 | Wyoming | 8.5 | South Carolina | 25.6 |
| Wisconsin | 5.1 | Massachusetts | 8.5 | Mississippi | 26.4 |
| Washington | 5.2 | Oklahoma | 8.9 | District of Columbia | 37.5 |

The results of these calculations offer another strong argument for Ohio as the most accurate bellwether over the last 30 elections. On average, Ohio's presidential vote deviated just 2.2 points from the national results. New Mexico, noted above as a historic bellwether, was second at 2.8 points.

The deviations calculated above track fairly well with the presidential win totals discussed above, with one major exception. While states like Ohio, New Mexico, Illinois, and Missouri lead this list—just as they do above—bellwether Nevada's vote has historically deviated much more strikingly over the last 30 elections, placing it in the middle of the pack of both tables 2.2 and 2.3.

Again, Nevada's strong support of silver bug Bryan, particularly in 1896 and 1900 at the start of this analysis, skews the numbers. Based on two-party vote, the Silver State was 33 points more Democratic than the nation in 1896, and 15 points more Democratic four years later. More recently, though, Nevada had presidential deviations of R +15, R +8, and R +7 in 1980, 1984, and 1988, respectively, before settling into a deviation near the national average moving into the 21st century.

If we narrow the time frame, Ohio's position as the leading bellwether becomes even more striking. Since 1964, Ohio has been at most just two points from the middle of the country either way, voting with the winner every time. Meanwhile, Illinois, the one-time battleground turned Democratic stronghold, has been at least five points more Democratic than the nation in every election since 1992. Missouri was four and seven points more Republican than the nation in 2008 and 2012, respectively, and was slightly more Republican in the three elections prior to that.

Using two-party presidential deviations can skew some state results. For instance, this method shows Alabama with a whopping R +52 deviation in 1948. Why? Because Truman was not even on the ballot there: conservative Democrat Strom Thurmond was on the ballot instead, so Truman got zero votes in Alabama. Thurmond won the all-party vote with nearly 80 percent, but Republican nominee Thomas Dewey got 100 percent of the two-party votes, or 52 points better than his national share of roughly 48 percent of the two-party tally. As is obvious, the two-party vote is not perfect, but when it performs poorly it is generally in the states of the South, which supported third-party candidates such as Thurmond in 1948 and Wallace in 1968. Nobody would consider those places bellwether states.

The District of Columbia, meanwhile, has never been less than 24 points more Democratic than the nation in its entire electoral history, which began in 1964. That gives it the highest average deviation from the nation's results of any place with electoral votes, by a significant margin.

Of all the other states (and DC), only two states besides Ohio have never been more than 10 points from the national voting since 1896: Ohio's neighbor to the west, Indiana, which is currently the most Republican state in the Midwest (and has been more Republican than the nation in every election since 1928), and historic bellwether Illinois, which is now the Midwest's consistently most Democratic state.

Averaging the presidential deviation over the last 30 elections helps confirm what Ohio's nearly flawless record in picking presidential winners suggests: Ohio is almost always reflective of the national popular vote. Its place in the middle of the national voting leads to a third argument for its importance as a presidential bellwether state. More often than any other state, Ohio puts the winning candidate over the finish line in the Electoral College.

OHIO: THE DECIDER

Technically, in 27 of the 30 elections from 1896 to 2012, the winning candidate still would have won without Ohio's electoral votes. The exceptions are 1916, 2000, and 2004. However, that statistic doesn't tell the full tale of how often Ohio votes close to the national average and how often it casts the decisive vote for the winner in both competitive and uncompetitive elections.

While Nevada and New Mexico have similar batting averages to Ohio's when it comes to voting with the winning presidential candidate, the Buckeye State has an obvious but nonetheless important advantage: it's always been much more populous than these far more sparsely populated western states. Ohio cast 18 electoral votes in 2012: while Ohio's number of electoral votes has been declining because of slow population growth, it was still the seventh highest in the nation, and Ohio has always ranked among the Electoral College's biggest prizes.

Nevada and New Mexico cast just six and five electoral votes, respectively, in 2012, and they've never cast more in any election. The small size of those two states means that they are not nearly as valuable to the candidates in terms of assembling a winning electoral coalition. They are too small, practically, to make the difference between winning and losing in all but the closest elections. Indeed, neither state has actually been decisive in the past 30 presidential elections.

Meanwhile, Ohio has produced the winning electoral vote for the victorious presidential candidate more times over the last 30 elections than any other state. In five of those elections, Ohio's electoral vote put the winner over the finish line.

Here's what that means: One can take the states that voted for the presidential winner and put them in order, from biggest margin to smallest, rather like Trende's hypothetical pool cited in chapter 1. Under this model, the state that produced the biggest percentage-point margin for the winner casts the first votes. For instance, in 2012, the District of Columbia voted for President Obama by an 83.6 percentage-point margin, by far the biggest margin won by either candidate that year in any place that cast electoral votes. So Obama got his "first" three electoral votes from DC. Obama's next four votes came from his birth state of Hawaii, which he won by 42.7 points. That put him at seven electoral votes. In that same election, Romney got his first six electoral votes from Utah, which he won by 47.9 points thanks to overwhelming support from his fellow Mormons (although Utah is frequently among the most Republican states in presidential elections). And so on. Once the winner gets to 270 electoral votes, the rest is gravy.

Table 2.4 lists the 30 elections from 1896 through 2012 and the "decisive" state in each election. In recent years, this means the 270th electoral

### Table 2.4. States providing decisive electoral vote, 1896–2012

| | | | | | |
|------|------------|------|--------------|------|--------------|
| 1896 | Ohio | 1936 | Ohio | 1976 | Wisconsin |
| 1900 | Illinois | 1940 | Pennsylvania | 1980 | Illinois |
| 1904 | New Jersey | 1944 | New York | 1984 | Michigan |
| 1908 | New York | 1948 | California | 1988 | Michigan |
| 1912 | New York | 1952 | Michigan | 1992 | Tennessee |
| 1916 | California | 1956 | Florida | 1996 | Pennsylvania |
| 1920 | Rhode Island | 1960 | Missouri | 2000 | Florida |
| 1924 | Utah | 1964 | Washington | 2004 | Ohio |
| 1928 | Illinois | 1968 | Ohio | 2008 | Iowa |
| 1932 | Iowa | 1972 | Ohio | 2012 | Colorado |

vote in the current Electoral College, which has 538 electoral votes, a total reached in 1964 with the addition of the District of Columbia and its three electoral votes.

Ohio cast this decisive vote five times: 1896 for Ohioan William McKinley, 1936 for Franklin Roosevelt, 1968 and 1972 for Richard Nixon, and 2004 for George W. Bush. The most recent instance was the most important: if Bush had lost Ohio in that close 2004 election, John Kerry would have been elected president. The other elections were not very competitive, except for 1968, which Nixon won by less than a point in the two-party vote over Hubert Humphrey.

No other state has cast decisive votes in more than three elections in this period: Illinois, Michigan, and New York each have been decisive three times. In fact, just 16 of the 50 states have cast the winning electoral votes in this 116-year period.

Additionally, Ohio has been just one slot away from being the crucial state five other times: 1900, 1948, 1964, 1976, and 1984. Included are two of the most competitive elections of the past century, Harry S. Truman's then-shocking upset of Thomas Dewey in 1948 and Jimmy Carter's near theft of defeat from the jaws of victory against hard-charging, unelected incumbent Gerald Ford in 1976.

In 1948, Truman won the national popular vote by about four and a half percentage points over Dewey, but Truman's victory was dependent on two very narrow escapes. One was in Ohio by a quarter of a point, and the other was in California by a little less than half a point. In 1976, Carter squeaked by in Ohio by about a quarter of a point, and in Wisconsin by less than two points. Later chapters will analyze these elections, and the candidates' performances in Ohio, in more depth.

Two key points: First, these statistics illustrate how Ohio is almost always near the national presidential voting, whether in very close elections (1968 and 2004) or in those that are not close at all (1936 and 1972). Second, the data also suggest that Ohio, because of its size, is more valuable to win than many other states. For all Nevada's and New Mexico's success in supporting the winner of presidential races, those two states have never during this 30-election span cast the decisive vote.

# Why Ohio?

Through Ohio's record of voting for the winning presidential nominee (28 times in the last 30 elections), its hewing to the national average (deviating an average of only 2.2 points from the country as a whole over those 30 elections), and its decisiveness in national elections (casting the winning votes more times than any other state), the Buckeye State has a strong claim as the most consistent and durable bellwether state over the last 30 presidential elections. The next logical question is: Why?

# THREE

## *Typical in All Things*

"Perhaps, as the social scientists say, we are only a national average, a convenient yard stick, typical in all things, singular in nothing," Harlan Hatcher writes in *The Buckeye Country*. Hatcher, an Ohio State University professor and fifth-generation Ohioan, did not agree with the assessment, though: "We Ohioans know that there is an illusive something more . . . the subtle X that colors our politics and religion; that gives tone to our big cities, and our country acres; that emanates from the college campuses and university halls; that broods over the hills of the Muskingum valley and over the lake shore and the plains; and we call it simply Ohio."[1]

From a political standpoint, figuring out that "subtle X" is crucial to understanding Ohio's presidential voting history. What is it about Ohio that places it so close to the national average in presidential elections? Is it something unique about the state—or is it something decidedly *non*-unique?

### OHIO'S REGIONS

Before exploring why the state mirrors the nation, it's first important to take a quick look at the state's politically and culturally diverse regions. The *Ohio Politics Almanac*, created by former *Columbus Dispatch* associate publisher Mike Curtin (who also has served in the state legislature as a Democrat), divides the state into six.

These regions are based in part on Ohio's media markets, which is very important in political campaigns because of the massive amounts of money each campaign and its allies spend on television advertising. The rise of targeted advertising through cell phones and Internet browsing may eventually make such media market distinctions less important, but as of the mid-2010s television advertising on broadcast and cable was still the primary way that campaigns reached voters.

Let's take a closer look at these six regions and how they voted from 2000 to 2012. While in 21st-century elections the state—like the nation—features a strong urban versus rural dynamic, with Republican candidates winning most of the counties but Democrats running strong in the state's most populated areas, there is a regional divide in the state as well, with the northeastern part of the state being the most Democratic and Republican strength lying in the western and southern portions of the state.

MAP 3.1. Ohio's six regions. *Source:* OhioElectionResults.com

Northeast: Anchored by Cleveland, this Rust Belt area is the state's electoral powerhouse. It casts the most votes, both Democratic and Republican, in state elections, and it's also the state's most Democratic region. Its two-party voting (57 percent Democratic) in 2000–2012 most resembled New Jersey, a reliably Democratic mid-Atlantic state. That's about six points more than the 51 percent going to the Democratic candidate in national two-party voting during the same period.

Northwest: The northwest features the city of Toledo, which is Democratic, as well as a few swing counties and then a number of bedrock GOP areas. Its voting (51 percent Democratic) most resembles Nevada's in recent elections, making it a swing region overall.

Central: Franklin County (Columbus) is the only county in this region that's very Democratic, but the state's most populous county's increasing lean toward the Party of Jackson makes the whole region competitive. It, too, is a swing region, but one that has been slightly less Democratic (49 percent) than the northwest over the last four elections, with voting that is most similar to Virginia's.

West: This small region based around Dayton is mostly conservative. At 57 percent Republican, its voting mirrors Louisiana's.

Southwest: Greater Cincinnati has long been the heart of Ohio Republicanism, even though Hamilton County, where Cincinnati is located, became a swing county in the 21st century. At an average of 58 percent Republican the past four elections, its voting is closest to Montana, a reliably Republican western state.

Southeast: An Appalachian band that runs along the Ohio River, the southeast casts by far the fewest votes of any of these six regions. It is historically competitive, but it trended away from Democrats in recent elections. At about 48 percent Democratic, its 2000–2012 voting mirrors Missouri, a state that was moving away from Democrats in a similar manner.

Another way to divide up the state, and one that state observers often cite, is the "Five Ohios" model, which folds Dayton in with the southwest and expands the size of the southeast, among other changes. Several political scientists from the University of Akron's Ray C. Bliss Institute of Applied Politics discuss the Five Ohios in their book *Buckeye Battleground*, an examination of Ohio voting and campaigns primarily focusing on races in the 2000s.[2] Whether one prefers to use five or six regions to divide the state, both methods do a good job of explaining the state's different areas.

One of the reasons that Ohio reflects the nation's political culture is because it features a diverse mix of the nation's political cultures. Ohio was not one of the original 13 states, but it entered the Union not long after the signing of the Constitution, becoming a state in 1803, about a decade and a half after the nation discarded the Articles of Confederation and elected its first president. The way Ohio was settled, though, predates statehood, and the roots planted by those earlier settlers arguably still affect the state's politics.

MAP 3.2. Ohio settlement patterns. *Source:* George Knepper, *Ohio and Its People,* Bicentennial Edition (Kent, OH: Kent State University Press, 2003), 55. Copyright © 2003 by The Kent State University Press. Reprinted by permission.

Much of the state's northeastern corner was part of the Western Reserve, starting on the state's eastern border and moving west along the Lake Erie shore toward the middle of the state. It contains Ashtabula (which some may recognize only for a throwaway mention in Bob Dylan's "You're Gonna Make Me Lonesome When You Go") and Youngstown, which doubles as the title of a Bruce Springsteen ode to the Rust Belt. It then moves west, covering Cleveland and Akron and also taking in cities like Elyria and Lorain as well as Oberlin and the liberal arts college that shares its name.

The Western Reserve was made up of lands claimed by Connecticut, which sold most of the land to a group of speculators, reserving the westernmost portion for people who had lost their homes in Connecticut to British raiders. This became known as the "Sufferers' Lands" or, in a term still used today, the "Firelands." Many towns in this part of the Western Reserve, like Norwalk and New London, are named for places in Connecticut.[3]

Settlement of these lands largely began in 1796 after the conclusion of wars with Native Americans. "The migration that started in that year was largely from New England," writes the Ohio master historian George Knepper in *Ohio and Its People*. "This fact gave a distinctly New England flavor to the Connecticut Reserve and has had a substantial impact upon the history of Ohio."[4] It was around this time that Moses Cleaveland, a member of the land company that bought the land from Connecticut, founded the city of Cleaveland (the first "a" was later dropped). The Ohio Company, another New England-oriented group, also led the settlement of a small part of southeast Ohio, which includes Ohio's first settlement, the quaint Ohio River town of Marietta, and Athens, home to Ohio University.

Virginia held a portion of land between the Scioto and Little Miami Rivers and north of the Ohio River (which forms the state's current southern border). This land, known as the Virginia Military District, was used "to pay bounties to soldiers who had served in the state's military forces."[5] This big blob of territory runs along the Ohio River from just outside Cincinnati to just west of Portsmouth, moving north to take in Chillicothe—Ohio's first capital—on its eastern border, and the western third of Franklin County, home of the current capital, Columbus, which is also the state's largest city.

"Residents of Virginia, Maryland, and Kentucky disproportionately populated the southern part of Ohio, particularly the Virginia Military District," write Kevin Kern and Gregory Wilson in *Ohio: A History of the Buckeye State*. Many of those southerners also populated the southeastern part of the state, "to the chagrin of some of its New Englander settlers."[6]

Overall, the state's first white settlers featured a mix of origins from across the young nation, with northeasterners largely settling in the northern part of the state, Middle Atlantic state natives in the middle, and southerners in the southern part. "More than any other state," Kern and Wilson write, "Ohio's population became a microcosm of the whole country due to migration patterns in the early statehood period."[7] Ohio arguably would remain a microcosm of the nation for its entire state history, not just because of its diverse foundations but also because it would change in ways that mirrored broader developments nationally.

The journalist Colin Woodard, in *American Nations: A History of the Eleven Rival Regional Cultures of North America*, shows how Ohio is one of the few states that has large sections that are part of three different American regional cultures. The Western Reserve is part of "Yankeedom," a culture that includes New England and most of New York. Other sections of the state are part of Woodard's "Midlands," which run from Pennsylvania through a sliver into the Midwest and the Great Plains, and "Greater Appalachia," which extends from western Pennsylvania and West Virginia all the way to northern Texas.

Woodard characterizes the history of North America as effectively a battle of ideas between Yankeedom (New England) and its allies versus the Deep South and Tidewater, allied with Greater Appalachia since the conclusion of the Civil War. The Midlands is "a bellwether for national political attitudes, and the key 'swing vote' in every national debate from the abolition of slavery to the 2008 presidential contest."[8] Woodard classifies about half of Ohio's 88 counties as Midlands. They form a band across the center and northwestern parts of the state, separating the Yankee Western Reserve in the northeast from the Greater Appalachian southwest and southeast.

Kern and Wilson's description of late-1800s politics suggests how Ohio's mixed regional roots positioned it in the nation's political middle: "In the late nineteenth century, sixteen states, mainly in the North, were reliably Republican and fourteen, mostly Southern, voted Democratic. That left a few states, Connecticut, New Jersey, New York, Indiana, Illinois and Ohio, as 'swing' states that could decide elections."[9] In a perpetual political battle between North and South, Ohio often found itself in the middle.

The battle would go on into the 21st century. The northeastern contingent has added the West Coast to its Upper Midwestern allies (now voting Democratic), while the southern forces can rely on Appalachia, the Great Plains, and the Interior West (voting Republican). The political party identifications may have changed over time, but the underlying ideologies—with the northeastern bloc more progressive and more comfortable with centralized power and the South more conservative and more suspicious of centralization—remain quite similar. Ohio is still in the middle, swaying back and forth to provide crucial support to one bloc or the other.

D. W. Meinig wrote in his multivolume *Shaping of America* series about how observers of western migration at the time predicted that the "moralistic" Yankees and "traditionalistic" Virginians who settled new lands like Ohio would enter into "some sort of convergence and blending of the two." However, Meinig argues, these observers overestimated "the ease and rapidity of blending and assimilation in America, . . . whereas in fact these regional, ethnic, and religious identities were fundamental and enduring."[10]

According to Woodard's breakdown of the regional cultures, the 16 states that entered the Union before Ohio belonged to the following categories:

- Connecticut, Massachusetts, New Hampshire, and Rhode Island were entirely part of Yankeedom.

- So was upstate New York, with the notable exception of New York City, which forms the heart of a different culture, New Netherland, a more diverse area that is politically bonded with the Yankee Northeast now but has not always been (New

York City was often supportive of the South before the Civil War, and Woodard noted that every New Netherland county supported Democrat Stephen Douglas over Republican Abraham Lincoln in the 1860 election).

- New Jersey is split between the New Netherland component and the Midlands. Pennsylvania has a little bit of Yankeedom, a little bit of Appalachia, and a lot of Midlands.

- Delaware, Maryland, and Virginia were mostly part of aristocratic, slaveholding "Tidewater," which extends down into northeastern North Carolina. Rounding out the original thirteen states are Georgia and South Carolina, part of the Deep South, a Tidewater ally.

- The three "new" states that entered before Ohio were Vermont—a Yankee enclave—and Kentucky and Tennessee, almost entirely part of Greater Appalachia.

The 17th state, Ohio, was different, featuring a mix of migrants from across the country and several distinct, competing regional cultures. Ohio is home to members of many different American cultural and political tribes, but it is dominated by none of them, which helps explain the state's political competitiveness, a trait that has defined the state for much of its history.

In its overview of the state for the New Deal–era American Guide Series (Hatcher, the author whose quote opened this chapter, edited that project), the Work Projects Administration's Writers' Program took notice of the state's mixed settlement: "These elements commingled, each affecting the other. And when in 1803, having the requisite population, Ohio became a State, it could be said, as of no other State at that time, that it was typically American." It adds: "Ohio is still as typically American as any State in the Union; it is neither North nor South, neither East nor West; it lies where they all meet and has characteristics and habits of all of them."[11]

A generation earlier, in an editorial celebrating the centennial of the founding of Ohio's permanent capital of Columbus in 1912, the *Cincinnati Times-Star* argued that "Ohio may be said to be the first true American State."[12]

While Ohio was settled by these distinctive cultures, surely the settlement patterns from more than two centuries ago cannot be relevant today? Actually, they just might be.

Although the Western Reserve was settled by a far more diverse group than just natives of Connecticut, the Nutmeg State has a strong connection to the area. Mike Dawson, a longtime Ohio Republican staffer and operative who maintains OhioElectionResults.com, has compiled a wonderful collection of Ohio voting stats. He breaks his results down both by counties and by regions, and those results indicate longstanding similarities in historical voting patterns between Connecticut and certain parts of Ohio.

One of those regions, the northeast, is a good proxy for the old Western Reserve. This region casts the most votes in presidential elections in the state—39 percent of the two-party votes in 2012—and it was the most Democratic, giving 57.6 percent of its two-party votes to Barack Obama, making it about six points more Democratic than the state as a whole that year.[13] This region contains the cities of Cleveland, Akron, Canton, and Youngstown. This definition of northeast Ohio extends a bit farther south than the actual Western Reserve boundaries, but it still fits well.

From 1896 to 2012, the voting patterns of northeast Ohio and Connecticut were strikingly similar. The correlation between their two-party votes was 0.84. To put that in perspective, a finding of 0 would indicate no relationship between the results while 1 would show a perfect relationship, so 0.84 means that the results were fairly closely correlated.

In several of the elections studied, both voted almost exactly the same. Both gave 65 percent of their votes to Republican Warren Harding in 1920. In 1932, FDR won northeast Ohio by a few hundredths of a percentage point but lost Connecticut by about a point. Neither place had much use for Republican Barry Goldwater in 1964: he won just 32 percent in each. The relationship is not deteriorating with time, either: from 1992 to 2012, Democratic presidential candidates won an average of 57.8 percent of the vote in northeast Ohio and 58.2 percent in Connecticut.

As Woodard observed, "the Yankee-settled portion of Ohio is evident on the county maps of the 2000 and 2004 elections: a strip of blue across the top of a largely red state."[14] Over two centuries of growth and demographic change, the Western Reserve started as Connecticut West—and, politically speaking, it remains as such.

Now, there is more at work here than just settlement patterns. Another part of the story is that both northeast Ohio and Connecticut attracted a large number of European immigrants throughout the early decades of the 20th century. In fact, the number of foreign-born white residents in both Connecticut and the major counties of the old Western Reserve is strikingly similar in census data throughout the early 20th century. These immigrants would help make both areas more Democratic after they had previously been more Republican. In other words, both Connecticut and what was effectively its colony shared similar roots, and over time they also changed in similar ways. Chapters 4 and 5 go into further detail about the effect these European immigrants had on Ohio politics and the state as a whole.

## Ohio's Issueless Politics

A classic study of Ohio's political culture comes from political scientist John H. Fenton's *Midwest Politics*. In the 1966 book, he described the state's politics as "issueless." His assessment of the Ohio electorate, especially compared to those of other midwestern states like Michigan, Minnesota, and Wisconsin, was harsh: "Ohio's politics cannot be understood without an appreciation of the generalized ignorance and indifference to government and politics on the part of Ohio's citizenry." The lack of interest by Ohioans in state politics, Fenton said, was in part because the parties failed to insert issues into campaigns, making them into popularity contests, or "pointless contests of personalities, devoid of meaningful issues."[15]

Without a dominant region or culture setting the tone for the state's politics, and with no ingrained political leanings, the state has produced leaders of all ideological stripes. While the state did produce eight presidents between 1840 and 1920 (none before or after), the Ohio presidents were by and large an undistinguished group.

- William Henry Harrison, born in Virginia, was the first winning Whig Party candidate, but he was not as obviously dedicated to the party's anti-Jacksonian "American System" of national internal improvements (i.e., infrastructure like roads and canals) as party stalwart Henry Clay, and he died soon after taking office, making it hard to judge how good or bad a president he would have been.

- Ulysses S. Grant is better remembered for his scandals in office than his support of the radical Republican Reconstruction program.

- Elected under a cloud of controversy, Rutherford B. Hayes oversaw the end of Reconstruction, which led to the resubjugation of blacks in the South.

- James A. Garfield was murdered before he could make an impact.

- Benjamin Harrison oversaw the passage of the Sherman Anti-Trust Act (named for Ohio Senator John Sherman, brother of General William Tecumseh Sherman) but is regarded by historians as only an average chief executive.

- William McKinley was perhaps the most consequential, if only because he stopped the candidacy of radical populist and Free Silver supporter William Jennings Bryan in 1896 and 1900 and ushered in an era of Republican dominance.

- William Howard Taft's presidency was sandwiched between two far-better-known and influential presidents, Theodore Roosevelt and Woodrow Wilson.

- Warren G. Harding was best remembered for scandal during his roughly two and a half years in the White House.

A recent ranking of the US presidents by members of the American Political Science Association, administered by Brandon Rottinghaus and Justin S. Vaughn, listed Taft (20) and McKinley (21) at roughly the middle of the pack of the 43 presidents, with every other Ohio president lower than them.[16]

More broadly, it's hard to argue that any of the Ohio presidents left a lasting, ideological mark on their respective parties (all were Republicans with the exception of William Henry Harrison, whose Whigs were effectively the precursor to the Republicans). McKinley probably comes the closest, but the GOP did not really emerge as both a pro-business and anti-government party until after World War I. To claim McKinley as the father of the modern GOP requires us to gloss over the Taft-Roosevelt faction fight in 1912 and the fact that the Republicans' growing devotion to laissez-faire capitalism and smaller government came in part as a reaction to what the party perceived as the excesses of both Wilson and, later, Franklin Delano Roosevelt.

So, the Ohio chief executives are the kinds of presidents one might expect a state with "issueless" politics to produce. The same can be said for the state's senators and governors, as a quick detour from this study of Ohio presidential results will demonstrate.

Many of the state's Democratic governors have been moderates or conservatives, like Frank Lausche, who served for 10 years in the 1940s and 1950s. In 1956, both parties considered him as a potential vice-presidential candidate, a sure sign that he was no liberal Democrat. That year, Ohioans sent him to the Senate, where he became one of its most conservative members. That his political career ended in a 1968 primary when he was strongly opposed by labor is a shorthand way of indicating his conservatism.

A generation earlier, Democrat Martin Davey spent much of his time in office during the Great Depression feuding with President Franklin Roosevelt's administration over the New Deal. More recently, Appalachian Democrat Ted Strickland rode into office during a 2006 national Democratic wave with the support of the National Rifle Association. Governors John Gilligan (1971–1975) and Richard Celeste (1983–1991) were more conventional liberals, but they also had help when they won: a loan scandal helped the Democratic ticket in 1970 after eight years of Republican rule, and Democrats had a strong midterm nationally in 1982 thanks in part to a recession that hit Ohio harder than most states. As a general rule, midterm elections are often bad for the party that holds the White House. For instance, the president's party lost ground in the US House in 36 of 39 midterm elections held from the end of the Civil War through the early 21st century. Turnout is usually about 15 to 20 points lower in midterms than in presidential elections, and typically the party that doesn't hold the White House is more motivated to vote, particularly if the incumbent president is unpopular or the national economy is poor. Starting in 1958, Ohio has elected governors to four-year terms in national midterm years—prior to that, governors were elected to two-year terms in even-numbered years—so national trends can bleed down the ballot and affect what happens in the state's gubernatorial races.

The two most noteworthy Ohio Republican governors of the second half of the 20th century were James A. Rhodes (1963–1971, 1975–1983) and George Voinovich (1991–1998). Rhodes, who was succeeded by the afore-mentioned Gilligan in 1971 and Celeste in 1983 (Rhodes narrowly beat the incumbent Gilligan in 1974 to start his second eight years in office), was a nonideological "jobs and progress" governor who relied on big, voter-approved bond issues. An Appalachian native schooled in popu-list politics, Rhodes played up his Appalachian roots whenever he got a chance. When speaking of his birthplace, Jackson County, Rhodes would quip that "a seven-course dinner down there is a possum and a six-pack."[17]

Voinovich is best known nationally as an occasional irritant to conser-vatives during his postgubernatorial 12 years in the US Senate (1999–2011). Republican John Kasich, who defeated Strickland in 2010 to claim the governorship, came into office as perhaps the most conservative governor of Ohio since the Democrat Lausche, according to the astute *Cleveland Plain Dealer* columnist Tom Suddes.[18] However, Kasich did not always govern that way: for instance, he upset some conservatives, but delighted the state's powerful health care establishment, by successfully pushing for an expansion of Medicaid made possible by the federal Affordable Care Act, better known as "Obamacare." Kasich ran for the 2016 Republican presidential nomination and was widely acknowledged as the candidate perhaps closest to the middle of all of his more than a dozen rivals. Kasich is no moderate, but he did not always govern as a strident conservative.

This is not to say that Ohio does not produce ideological leaders. The state's senators in the first half of the 2010s, liberal Democrat Sher-rod Brown and conservative Republican Rob Portman, were not mod-erates. Rather, it's more accurate to say that the state has not produced ideologically consistent Democrats and Republicans. Strong liberals and conservatives can win in Ohio when circumstances allow, but there's no ideological rhyme or reason that suggest the next strong liberal or strong conservative that follows in that person's footsteps will be as successful. In fact, many of Ohio's major statewide elected officials have been strongly ideological. Their victories, however, seemed due less to strong ideological choices by the voters and more to being in the right place at the right time.

Conservative Republican Senator John W. Bricker, a former governor and Republican presidential nominee Thomas Dewey's running mate in 1944, first won his Senate seat in 1946, a midterm year where Republicans netted 13 Senate and 56 House seats nationally and won control of both the House and Senate for the first time since 1928. Bricker comfortably won reelection in 1952, when Dwight Eisenhower's strong performance at the top of the ticket helped the GOP narrowly retake the House and Senate.

In 1958, Bricker seemed like a good bet to win a third term against a liberal Democrat, Stephen Young. But amidst a national depression and a foolish push by conservatives to make Ohio a "right to work" state in order to weaken Democratic-leaning labor unions, Democrats had a great year in both Ohio and the nation, allowing Young to defeat Bricker. Six years later, President Lyndon Johnson's one-million-vote win over Republican Barry Goldwater created the lift that allowed for Young's 17,000-vote squeaker reelection over Republican Robert Taft Jr., son of the legendary Senator Robert A. Taft and father of Bob Taft, the Ohio governor from 1999 to 2007. Young didn't run for reelection in 1970, allowing Taft Jr. to win the seat, which he held for a single term before losing in 1976 to liberal Democrat Howard Metzenbaum, who unseated Taft while Jimmy Carter was narrowly carrying Ohio.

Brown and Portman also benefited from good timing in their victories. Brown defeated Republican Senator Mike DeWine in 2006 in the midst of the aforementioned national Democratic wave that also helped Strickland win the governorship. Brown won his second term in 2012, helped by both President Obama's reelection victory—Obama and Brown won almost the exact same share of the vote—and the underwhelming Republican campaign of State Treasurer Josh Mandel, who ran several points behind Republican presidential nominee Mitt Romney, ceding votes to little-known third-party candidates.

Portman, meanwhile, ran to replace the retiring Voinovich in an optimal year to run as a Republican, 2010, when the GOP netted 63 seats in the House and six Senate seats. Hapless Democratic Senate nominee Lee Fisher, the state's lieutenant governor, ran an inert campaign that hardly pushed Portman.

This is not to say that Ohio's down-ballot results always reflect the national trends. DeWine (2000) and Voinovich (2004), for instance, won uncompetitive reelections in years that were very close at the presidential level in Ohio (though their fellow Republican, George W. Bush, won Ohio in both elections). The power of incumbency and outmatched Democratic opponents easily explains the discrepancy. Campaigns do matter, after all, especially when one side has a lot of resources and prestige and the other does not.

In 1988, Metzenbaum easily defeated then-Cleveland Mayor Voinovich to win a third term while Republican George H. W. Bush cruised to victory in the Buckeye State and nationally. But that was not an odd result nationally that year, which featured the second-lowest correlation between presidential and Senate results in any presidential year since the popular election of senators began nationwide in 1914.[19] Bush's big national win was a "lonely landslide" where Republicans gained no ground in the Senate and actually lost three net House seats. Just 10 House or Senate incumbents lost that year, observed Ross K. Baker in *The Election of 1988*, and those who did fell into three categories: "the unlucky, the inept, and the venal."[20] Metzenbaum was none of those things in 1988, and Voinovich ran a widely panned race. So, in producing a divergent presidential and Senate result in 1988, Ohio was still very much in line with the rest of the country that year.

Of all the Ohio politicos over the decades, Ray Bliss had perhaps the best advice for candidates. Bliss served as state Republican Party chairman from 1949 to 1965. He then took over the Republican National Committee chairmanship after the disastrous 1964 election, when Goldwater's horrible performance had left the party in shambles. The quintessential party man, Bliss cared only about winning: "Ray has no ideological convictions—at least none that he's ever mentioned to me—and so nobody's against him," one Republican said of him after he became the national party chairman.[21] Bliss's advice? "Keep issues out of campaigns." His aphorism inspired Fenton's description of the state's politics, noted at the beginning of this section.

## No Dominant Cities

Want to know the difference between Ohio, a bellwether state, and Illinois, a Democratic one?

In the 2012 election, Cook County (Chicago) cast just a shade over two million votes, or 38 percent of all the presidential votes in Illinois. Ohio's three most populous counties—Cuyahoga (Cleveland), Franklin (Columbus), and Hamilton (Cincinnati)—together cast about 1.6 million votes, or 29 percent of the state's total. Obama won Cook County 74 percent to 25 percent (all-party voting) over Romney, and won the counties of Ohio's "three Cs" major cities 62 percent to 37 percent.

Take out Cook County from the results, and Romney wins Illinois 51 percent to 47 percent. Take out Cuyahoga, Franklin, and Hamilton from Ohio, and Romney wins 52 percent to 46 percent. So, outside of those major urban counties—just one in Illinois and three in Ohio—they are, electorally speaking, effectively the same state. The difference is that Chicago and its closest suburbs pack a bigger electoral punch than Cleveland, Columbus, and Cincinnati and their closest suburbs combined, and Illinois's dominant urban county is more Democratic than all three of Ohio's put together: Obama, respectively, won 69 percent in Cuyahoga, 61 percent in Franklin, and 53 percent in Hamilton.

Cuyahoga, which despite years of population loss still has cast the most votes of any county in the state in every election since 1916, produced only about 12 percent of the state's ballots in 2012. Obviously, that's a small number compared to Cook County, which produced 38 percent of Illinois's. Even Wayne County (Detroit), another struggling, declining county, cast 17 percent of Michigan's votes in 2012. Milwaukee County cast 16 percent of Wisconsin's votes; Hennepin County (Minneapolis but not St. Paul) cast 23 percent. The five counties that make up New York

City's five boroughs cast 35 percent of New York's votes, about equivalent to Cook County's share of the Illinois vote.

The difference between Ohio and Illinois—and many other states—is that Ohio does lack and has always lacked a dominant urban center. And, as we'll explore in further detail later in the book, Ohio's cities have hardly been uniformly Democratic. Since about the time of the Great Depression, Cuyahoga County has been consistently more Democratic than the state and nation, while Franklin and Hamilton had been, for most of the 20th century, more Republican. None of these counties dominates the state voting, and each will often vote in different ways from the other two.

## No Dominant Industries or Issues

In October 2015, businessman Donald Trump was leading virtually every national and state-level poll of the Republican presidential primary, except, notably, in Iowa. Neurosurgeon Ben Carson, a favorite of the state's heavily white, evangelical, caucus-going electorate, had taken a mid-single-digit lead in polling averages there. Trump, who had been bragging about how good his polling was since entering the race in mid-June, took a shot at the first-in-the-nation caucus electorate by retweeting a comment from one of the followers of his widely read Twitter account: "#BenCarson is now leading in the #polls in #Iowa. Too much #Monsanto in the #corn creates issues in the brain? #Trump #GOP." Monsanto, based in Missouri, is an agrochemical giant.

The tweet caused an immediate stir. "Is Trump going after Iowans now?" tweeted Jennifer Jacobs, the influential *Des Moines Register*'s top political reporter.[22] It became yet another Trump cause célèbre, keeping him in the headlines for another day.

Trump had spent the whole summer and into the fall saying all sorts of offensive things, many of them far more noteworthy than the Iowa tweet. He had questioned the heroism of Republican Senator John McCain of Arizona, a Vietnam war–era prisoner of war ("I like people who weren't captured").[23] He had insulted the looks of Carly Fiorina, the former Hewlett-Packard CEO who was also running for the GOP nomination ("Look at that face! Would anyone vote for that? Can you imagine that, the face of our next president?!").[24] He got in several tiffs with Megyn Kelly, the Fox News Channel host.

While Trump made an effort to wiggle his way out of several of these comments after the fact, saying he had been misquoted or misunderstood, he devised a new excuse for his Iowa insult: "The young intern who accidentally did a Retweet apologizes." That Trump felt the need to resort to blaming staff for this insult, when he effectively took ownership of many of his other previous outrageous comments, shows that even Trump knew that, when it came to Iowa, making jokes about agriculture was simply a line he couldn't cross. (Trump would finish second in the 2016 Iowa caucus before winning several subsequent nominating contests.)

Iowa is known as an agriculture state, and it defines the state's political culture, even as the number of Iowans who work in agriculture was declining in the 21st century.[25] The agriculture industry is so important to Iowa's political identity that it can occasionally cause the state to make political decisions that it might otherwise not make.

In 1988, George H. W. Bush handily defeated Michael Dukakis, beating him by roughly eight points nationally and rolling up a 426–111 advantage in the Electoral College. The Dukakis states were a small collection of the nation's most Democratic-leaning states, like Hawaii, Massachusetts, and New York. And yet Dukakis performed better in Iowa than in any of those states: he won it with 54.7 percent of the all-party vote, the Democrat's third-best showing anywhere in the nation, behind only the District of Columbia and Rhode Island. In the two-party vote, Iowa's presidential deviation that year was D +9, the most Democratic the state has ever been in the current two-party era. What happened?

A farm crisis. The state's "farm economy has been battered during the Reagan years in office," the *Washington Post* noted in a postelection explanation of the results.[26] Dukakis performed better than one might otherwise expect in both Iowa and several other states, winning Minnesota (reliably Democratic) and Wisconsin (more of a swing state in most elections) in part because of this farm crisis. Even though Bush easily carried them, his performance in agriculture-heavy states like Kansas and Nebraska was also several points weaker than might be expected. Meanwhile, Ohio was right in the middle of the nation again that year—the state's presidential deviation was actually R +2. Agriculture may be "the strongest industry in Ohio," as Governor Kasich said in 2012 (a statement verified by the fact-checkers of PolitiFact),[27] but the state is economically diverse enough that fluctuations in one industry have not led to out-of-the-ordinary presidential election results.

Ohio is a major producer of agricultural goods, but it is not an agriculture state like Iowa. Ohio produces a lot of cars, but it is not an auto state like Michigan, where the big three American automakers (General Motors, Ford, and Chrysler) are based. Ohio has a lot of natural resources, but it is not a coal state like West Virginia. It contains all of these industries, but it is not defined by any single one of them. While it's easy for elites on the coasts to dismiss Ohio and its midwestern neighbors as "flyover country," only the most ignorant would think to classify Ohio as a farm state. It's of course possible to insult Ohioans as a bloc—perhaps by saying something nasty about the state's collective obsession, the Ohio State University football team—but the state's economy is so diverse, and has been so diverse for so long, that economic identity politics are not a major part of the state's political culture.

The state mirrors the nation in other ways. Ohio urbanized faster than the nation as a whole, but for the last half century the state's urban/rural population split—consistently about 75 percent urban and 25 percent rural—has effectively mirrored the national trends. Unemployment rates have also mirrored the nation's for decades, with the exception of a bigger spike than the national average throughout the 1980s as a wave of industrial stagnation hit the nation, dramatically affecting parts of manufacturing-heavy Ohio and sending parts of the state, such as the Youngstown area, into a condition of economic paralysis that never truly healed. In 1960, more than half of the state's employment was in manufacturing, but by the 2010s barely over a tenth of it was. The service industry now dominates employment (close to half of all jobs are in services).

The state's Fortune 500 companies as of 2015 were as follows, in order of size: Kroger, Marathon Petroleum, Cardinal Health, Procter and Gamble, Nationwide, Macy's, Progressive, Goodyear Tire and Rubber, American Electric Power, FirstEnergy, Parker Hannifin, L Brands, Sherwin-Williams, TravelCenters of America, Owens-Illinois, Dana

Holding, Omnicare, AK Steel Holding, Fifth Third Bancorp, American Financial Group, J. M. Smucker, Western & Southern Financial Group, and Owens Corning. That's a diverse group, featuring a variety of energy companies, insurers, banks, manufacturers, and retailers. And that doesn't include the state's public sector and nonprofit employers, like Ohio's many colleges and universities as well as its hospitals, an impressive list led by the Cleveland Clinic. Ohio is not just a cultural and political melting pot—it's an economic one, too.

With no dominant industry and no dominant, unique political problem that defines its voting, Ohio has simply moved with the national tides. It has been largely immune to regional disruptions that have caused other states with narrower interests to produce outlier results. For instance, it has never supported a third-party candidate for president, unlike many states of the South, which backed the segregationist Dixiecrats Strom Thurmond in 1948 and George Wallace in 1968 because those states' politics were (are?) so dominated by race.

Wallace got plenty of votes in Ohio, just as he did everywhere, but not nearly enough to win the state or even a single county. In that, he was just like every other third-party candidate in Ohio over the past hundred years—the last one to win even a single Ohio county was Teddy Roosevelt in the great GOP schism election of 1912. No, Ohio prefers just Democrats or Republicans, just like most of the rest of the country.

### The Testing Ground

In the high security test kitchen at Wendy's International, they're working on what they hope will be the next big thing: the Black Label Burger. But don't start drooling just yet. Before it goes to your town, it first has to make the grade here: Columbus, Ohio.

—CBS News, June 24, 2012

Columbus is a bellwether for reasons beyond just politics. It has long been a test market for products, in past decades because its demographics mirrored the nation's and, more recently, because the city features a number of different kinds of consumers that marketers value, like college students and single people living on their own. "It's Middle America," CBS reported, "but that doesn't mean it's *average*."[28]

George Knepper, the Ohio historian, answers the question posed at the start of the chapter: Is the state unique, or non-unique? "States love to boast of their unique aspects, but Ohio's claim to fame is the antithesis of uniqueness."[29]

Ohio is special because, in so many political and nonpolitical ways, it is not special.

So, every four years, the political parties send their products for testing in the Buckeye State. If the product doesn't sell there, chances are it won't sell nationally, either.

# FOUR

## *The Civil War at the Ballot Box, 1896–1932*

Ohio held perhaps its most peculiar election in the midst of the Civil War. Its results help explain the voting patterns that emerged later, when the state began its best-in-the-nation streak of voting for the presidential winner more than three decades later, in 1896.

In 1863, the Ohio Democratic Party nominated an unusual candidate for governor. While there was nothing odd or particularly noteworthy about Clement Vallandigham's qualifications for office—he was a former member of the US and Ohio Houses of Representatives—there was something very strange about his place of residence during the campaign: he ran for governor from exile in Canada.

Vallandigham was a leader of Ohio's Peace Democrats, a group of antiwar and anti-Lincoln Democrats "whose state rights constitutionalism had been outraged by the war-time acts of the Lincoln administration," as Eugene Roseboom described them in *The History of the State of Ohio.*[1] Unionists called these Peace Democrats "Copperheads," equating them to venomous snakes slithering among them.

Vallandigham believed in the preservation of slavery and readmission of the South to the Union. Despite a Democratic surge in Ohio in the 1862 midterm election, Vallandigham lost his southwest Ohio US House seat. Vallandigham—described by Roseboom as "one of the most courageous, strong-willed, and wrong-headed men in Ohio's history"[2]—was undaunted, and he plotted a run for governor in 1863.

General Ambrose Burnside, who after presiding over a Union defeat at the Battle of Fredericksburg took command of the Union army's Department of the Ohio, headquartered in Cincinnati, "was annoyed at the southern sympathies and even treasonous activities of some elements of that city and determined to curb them." He issued an order that forbade "declaring sympathy for the enemy."[3] Vallandigham, "courting a martyrdom to advance his quest for Ohio's governorship," spoke against the order, and Burnside had him arrested.[4]

Lincoln, the first president from what is today's Republican Party, exiled Vallandigham to the Confederacy, where he was not really welcome, because "to accept him would indict the Peace Democrats as being pro-Confederate." With Confederate help he made his way to Canada, where from the shores of the Detroit River he stood as the Democratic nominee for governor of Ohio. John Brough, the nominee of the Union Party (effectively the rebranded Republicans), defeated Vallandigham by about 100,000 votes, or 60 percent to 40 percent, in the general election, prompting Lincoln to wire Brough the morning after the election and express his relief at the outcome: "Glory to God in the Highest, Ohio has saved the Union."[5]

Vallandigham won just 19 of the 88 counties, his strength concentrated in the central and northwestern parts of the state. Brough ran up big margins in the old Western Reserve, and he also comfortably carried Hamilton County (Cincinnati), which cast about 8 percent of the total two-party votes in that election, or more than double the votes of any other county.

Election analysts should not overinterpret the results of midterm elections when trying to predict the next presidential election, but in this case the 1863 election results strongly foreshadowed what was to come a year later, when Lincoln himself would stand for reelection against Democrat George McClellan, a former commander of the Union army who had begun the war commanding the Ohio militia. McClellan's running mate was George Pendleton, a member of the US House from Cincinnati and, like Vallandigham, a Peace Democrat.

Lincoln won 55 percent to McClellan's 45 percent nationally and 56 percent to 44 percent in Ohio. McClellan outperformed Vallandigham in the state by a few points, but otherwise their areas of strength (central and northwest) and weakness (northeast, southeast, and southwest) were about the same. That's unsurprising given that these were two contentious elections contested during wartime. Vallandigham had reentered the United States by this time—Lincoln decided to ignore him—and attended the 1864 Democratic convention as a delegate.[6]

What's fascinating about the results of the elections of 1863 and 1864 is that they would remain relevant in Ohio's voting patterns after the Civil War and into the 20th century, so that in the election of 1896—the election where Ohio began its streak of going through 30 elections (and counting) while voting only twice for the presidential loser—the state's electoral alignment had not changed much from 30-plus years prior. The correlation at the county level between Vallandigham's 1863 results and Democrat William Jennings Bryan's 1896 numbers is a strong 0.87 (again, 0 means no relationship, and 1 means a perfect relationship) and an even stronger 0.89 when comparing the 1864 results to those of 1896.

The postwar electoral landscape reflected the politics of wartime: the North remained largely Republican, the South remained solidly Democratic, and a few states in the middle with split political personalities, like Ohio, remained in play. The county-level party loyalties that prevailed during the Civil War were still evident at the dawn of the 20th century.

An example is Holmes County, which in 1896 was the most Democratic county in Ohio. It is also one of the least typical. Holmes, located about 80 miles south of Cleveland, is the heart of Ohio's Amish Country and home to the largest concentration of Amish in the world. Holmes was a hotbed of resistance to the Civil War. A group of residents actually organized to fight federal troops to protest the draft, but the resisters were quickly dispersed and no one was killed in the fighting.

In 1863, Holmes County was Vallandigham's second-best county in the state. Mercer, another rural county in the western part of the state, was narrowly his best. The Vallandigham counties could be categorized in three ways, according to Kevin Phillips in his 1969 book, *The Emerging Republican Majority*:

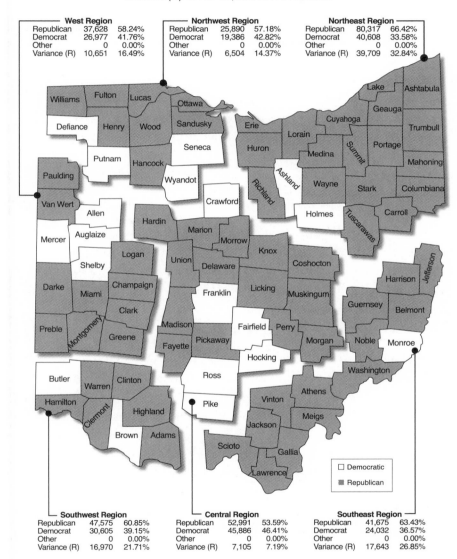

**1863 Ohio Governor's Race**

| | | |
|---|---|---|
| *Brough (R) | 286,076 | 60.41% |
| Vallandigham (D) | 187,494 | 39.59% |
| Other | 0 | 0.00% |
| Variance (R) | 98,582 | 20.82% |

**West Region**

| | | |
|---|---|---|
| Republican | 37,628 | 58.24% |
| Democrat | 26,977 | 41.76% |
| Other | 0 | 0.00% |
| Variance (R) | 10,651 | 16.49% |

**Northwest Region**

| | | |
|---|---|---|
| Republican | 25,890 | 57.18% |
| Democrat | 19,386 | 42.82% |
| Other | 0 | 0.00% |
| Variance (R) | 6,504 | 14.37% |

**Northeast Region**

| | | |
|---|---|---|
| Republican | 80,317 | 66.42% |
| Democrat | 40,608 | 33.58% |
| Other | 0 | 0.00% |
| Variance (R) | 39,709 | 32.84% |

**Southwest Region**

| | | |
|---|---|---|
| Republican | 47,575 | 60.85% |
| Democrat | 30,605 | 39.15% |
| Other | 0 | 0.00% |
| Variance (R) | 16,970 | 21.71% |

**Central Region**

| | | |
|---|---|---|
| Republican | 52,991 | 53.59% |
| Democrat | 45,886 | 46.41% |
| Other | 0 | 0.00% |
| Variance (R) | 7,105 | 7.19% |

**Southeast Region**

| | | |
|---|---|---|
| Republican | 41,675 | 63.43% |
| Democrat | 24,032 | 36.57% |
| Other | 0 | 0.00% |
| Variance (R) | 17,643 | 26.85% |

☐ Democratic
▨ Republican

Map 4.1. The 1863 Ohio gubernatorial election.
*Note:* Asterisk denotes election winner. *Source:* OhioElectionResults.com

- Substantially German Catholic and rural, like the aforementioned Mercer County in the west and its neighbors Auglaize, Allen, and Shelby Counties, as well as some northwest counties; or

- Settled by the Pennsylvania Dutch, such as the Amish. Holmes County and its northwestern neighbor, Ashland, are examples, as is Fairfield, which lies southeast of Columbus and has as its county seat Lancaster, named for the Pennsylvania town and county from which so many of its earliest residents came (Fairfield County gave McClellan 59 percent of the vote in 1864, even as the county's famous native son, William Tecumseh Sherman, was laying waste to the South); or

- Southern-settled counties in the central and southwestern parts of the state, like Franklin County (Columbus) and Butler County (home of Miami University, north of Cincinnati).

According to Phillips, what tied these disparate elements together was that, while they did not necessarily have a love for slavery, "they could not stand Yankees."[7] The Republicans were the party of the Yankees, both during the Civil War and for decades after.

## McKinley and Rock-Ribbed Republicanism, 1896–1908

Nearly 35 years after strongly backing Vallandigham, Holmes County's presidential deviation was D +26, making it Democratic nominee William Jennings Bryan's best county in the state. It was one of many rural counties that loved Bryan, including Mercer, which was D +23 and provided Bryan's second-best showing.

Unfortunately for Bryan, hills, trees, and rocks cannot vote. The state's most populous counties generally preferred William McKinley, the Republican nominee, who ran for president from his home in Canton, Ohio. McKinley's strength was concentrated in the northeastern and southern parts of the state. Hamilton County, which at the turn of the century continued to cast the most votes in the state, went strongly for McKinley (R +8). Cuyahoga County (Cleveland), which cast the second-most votes, also backed McKinley, but it was only a point more Republican than the state as a whole. The same was true of Franklin County, which cast the third-most votes and voted about the same way as the state overall.

Of the nine counties that cast more than 15,000 total votes in the election, McKinley carried them all. Altogether, he won 38,780 more votes in these counties than Bryan did, about 80 percent of his 48,494-vote margin.

Ohio in the 1890s reflected the national voting results, and it was similar to the nation in other ways. Throughout much of the 19th century, Ohio, like the United States, experienced a wave of European immigration, particularly from Ireland and Germany. Still, in the 1890 census, Ohio's population was 87 percent native-born, quite similar to the nation's 85 percent. Of Ohio's foreign-born population in 1890, roughly half were German, and close to a third were from the British Isles, primarily from Ireland and England.

About a third of Ohio residents in 1890 had a foreign parent, however. While that percentage may seem high, it tallied with that of the nation as a whole and was the lowest of any midwestern state other than Indiana. By comparison, in newer Upper Midwest states like Minnesota and Wisconsin, about three-quarters of residents had a foreign-born parent in 1890. Ohio's biggest cities, Cincinnati and Cleveland, were dominated by immigrants or the children of immigrants: 70 percent of Cincinnatians had a foreign parent, as did 75 percent of Clevelanders. These were mainly Germans and Irish.

The southern United States, meanwhile, had few European immigrants, but it did have the lion's share of the nation's African Americans: more than 90 percent of the nation's black population lived in the former slave states of the South and the Border States of Delaware, Kentucky, Maryland, and Missouri. Throughout the latter stages of the 19th century, however, these citizens experienced Jim Crow's slow erosion of the voting rights they had won after the end of slavery and the Civil War.

While Ohio eventually gained a sizeable African American community, it accounted for only 2.4 percent of the state's population, according to the US Census of 1890. African Americans were scattered throughout the state, but close to a fifth lived in Hamilton County, and another 10 percent resided in Clark and Greene Counties between Columbus and Dayton.

Greene County is home to Wilberforce University, the oldest private historically black college in the United States. In 1890, about 14 percent of the county's total population was black, the highest percentage in the state. Black voters then were still mostly Republican, in allegiance to Abraham Lincoln and the forces of emancipation. The county strongly supported McKinley in 1896, but its Republicanism dated back long before that election. It strongly supported Brough in the 1863 gubernatorial race, at which time blacks were forbidden to vote in Ohio. Only the passage of the 15th Amendment, which gave voting rights to blacks across the country, allowed black suffrage in Ohio, and even then the state's constitution retained a black voting prohibition into the 20th century, though it had been rendered moot. Institutionalized racism, sadly, was not and is not just a southern phenomenon.

To put in perspective how overwhelmingly white the north was in 1890, Greene County had the highest percentage of black residents of any county above the Mason-Dixon Line, the old political barrier that delineated slave states from free states.[8] Even with its paltry black population in 1890, Ohio's percentage of black residents was still higher than nearly every other non-Confederate or non-Border State.

Overall, in 1896 McKinley handily won the state's northeast, southeast, and southwest regions. Bryan narrowly carried central Ohio and the northwest, and the west backed McKinley.

Four years later, McKinley and Bryan fought a rematch, and the state- and county-level results were much the same. Once again, the Republican share of the state's two-party vote was almost exactly the same as the national vote, the only real difference being that McKinley won a few counties in the northwest and central parts of the state that he had previously lost. The correlation between the 1896 and 1900 Democratic two-party vote is 0.98, indicating an almost perfect relationship between the two results.

McKinley was murdered early in his second term by Leon Czolgosz, an anarchist. Theodore Roosevelt, the former governor of New York, became president. This was much to the chagrin of Ohio senator Mark Hanna, the Republican political fixer who had guided McKinley to the White House and who had vehemently opposed Roosevelt's selection as

# 1896 Ohio Presidential Election

| | | |
|---|---|---|
| *McKinley (R) | 525,991 | 51.86% |
| Bryan (D) | 474,882 | 46.82% |
| Other | 13,422 | 1.32% |
| Variance (R) | 51,109 | 5.04% |

**West Region**

| | | |
|---|---|---|
| Republican | 73,942 | 49.46% |
| Democrat | 73,567 | 49.21% |
| Other | 1,987 | 1.33% |
| Variance (R) | 375 | 0.25% |

**Northwest Region**

| | | |
|---|---|---|
| Republican | 57,168 | 46.74% |
| Democrat | 63,520 | 51.93% |
| Other | 1,633 | 1.34% |
| Variance (D) | 6,352 | 5.19% |

**Northeast Region**

| | | |
|---|---|---|
| Republican | 152,816 | 53.73% |
| Democrat | 127,460 | 44.81% |
| Other | 4,162 | 1.46% |
| Variance (R) | 25,356 | 8.91% |

☐ Democratic
■ Republican

**Southwest Region**

| | | |
|---|---|---|
| Republican | 87,094 | 55.50% |
| Democrat | 68,377 | 43.58% |
| Other | 1,441 | 0.92% |
| Variance (R) | 18,717 | 11.93% |

**Central Region**

| | | |
|---|---|---|
| Republican | 91,344 | 48.58% |
| Democrat | 94,259 | 50.13% |
| Other | 2,433 | 1.29% |
| Variance (D) | 2,915 | 1.55% |

**Southeast Region**

| | | |
|---|---|---|
| Republican | 63,627 | 56.26% |
| Democrat | 47,699 | 42.18% |
| Other | 1,766 | 1.56% |
| Variance (R) | 15,928 | 14.08% |

MAP 4.2. The 1896 presidential election in Ohio. *Source:* OhioElectionResults.com

the GOP's vice-presidential nominee at the 1900 Republican convention. After Roosevelt was added to the ticket, Hanna told McKinley that his "duty to the country is to live for four years from next March."[9] McKinley barely made it six months into his new term.

Roosevelt went on to an easy 1904 victory both nationally and in Ohio, improving on McKinley's performances in his home state and pushing the state to an R +4 presidential deviation against Democrat Alton Parker, chief judge of the New York state appeals court.

Four years later, Bryan ran a third time, and for the third time he faced an Ohioan in the general election, Secretary of War William Howard Taft. The two-party vote was very similar to that of McKinley's battles with Bryan: Ohio almost exactly mirrored the nation once again, although it was one point more Democratic.

These four elections display a high level of continuity. Of Ohio's 88 counties, 50 voted for the winning Republicans in all four elections, including the three that cast the most votes: Cuyahoga, Franklin, and Hamilton. Another 16 voted Democratic in all four, which means that three-quarters of the state's counties were locked into partisan identities throughout the period.

One of the four-time Democratic counties was Ottawa, a small county just east of Toledo. In the 1900 census, Ottawa had the highest percentage of residents who had been born in Germany of any Ohio county (16 percent). People of German descent were a key part of the Democratic coalition, and new immigrants in general had flocked to the Democrats for decades, dating back to Andrew Jackson and the founding of the party. Many of the northwest and central Ohio counties had significant German populations, and among their gripes with the Republicans was that party's association with the forces supporting Prohibition: Germans on both sides of the Atlantic love their beer. The Irish, a smaller immigrant group in Ohio, felt much the same way and voted Democratic.

These groups, however, lacked the strength to get their way in presidential elections in Ohio. As of 1908, the Republican Party had fielded a presidential candidate in 14 elections going back to 1856, won 11 of them, and carried Ohio in all. That success changed in 1912, when the GOP was torn asunder.

After winning in 1904, Roosevelt made a pledge that he would come to regret, promising not to seek a second elected term. Instead, he backed Taft. But Roosevelt's desire to be president endured, and he grew disappointed in what he considered his successor's conservatism. So Roosevelt challenged Taft for the GOP nomination in 1912. Taft defeated him because his forces maintained control of the party's convention, so Roosevelt immediately launched a third-party candidacy under the banner of the Progressive ("Bull Moose") Party.

The GOP split allowed Democrat Woodrow Wilson to capture the White House easily, while only winning about 42 percent of the national vote. Roosevelt (27 percent) finished ahead of Taft (23 percent) and Socialist Party candidate Eugene Debs (6 percent).

Ohio gave Wilson 41 percent, nearly the same as the nation as a whole, but essentially reversed Taft and Roosevelt's national performance, giving the Ohioan 27 percent and the New Yorker 22 percent. Roosevelt ran best in the Western Reserve, perhaps foreshadowing the region's eventual turn to what became the more progressive party, the Democrats. Taft, meanwhile, performed most strongly in his native southwest. Wilson won a majority of the vote in just 17 counties, none of which cast more than 10,000 total votes (all having relatively small populations) and all of which had voted for McClellan a half century earlier. Their candidate had lost during the nation's Civil War, but these counties found themselves on the winning side after the Republican Civil War of 1912.

Four years later, Wilson stood for reelection, this time opposed by a Republican Party unified around Charles Evans Hughes, a former governor of New York and member of the US Supreme Court. The reunited Republicans sought to prove that Ohio's turn to the Democrats had been just a fluke.

By mid-October, however, the *Chicago Daily Tribune*'s Arthur Sears Henning reported that, surprisingly, the Republicans were getting nervous. "Ohio is giving the politicians a novel experience. It is a doubtful state for the first time within the memory of the men who are running the Republican and Democratic campaigns." Remember: while Ohio's vote had closely tracked the national average for decades, the Democrats had been unable at any point (except 1912) to pry it from the GOP. Henning noted the strength of the Ohio economy and Wilson's solid lead in the northeastern part of the state, due in part to gangbusters war munitions production centered in that industrial region (World War I was raging in Europe at the time, but the United States was still a bystander). National economic growth was strong in 1916 and probably was a key reason for Wilson's winning a second term in an otherwise Republican-leaning era. So, too, was the budding power of unions, which strongly backed Wilson. And, most important, Wilson had "kept the country out of war," as a Democrat running the campaign in Cleveland told Henning, proving that he understood the power of staying on message in a tough campaign: Wilson's neutrality in the war was his strongest selling point. By 1916, the bellicose Roosevelt was back in the GOP fold and was agitating for war, a move that alienated German American voters. "We are telling the Germans that Roosevelt will be in Hughes' cabinet," a Democrat told Henning. "It is quite effective, I think."[10]

Henning's report was prophetic when it came to northeast Ohio. Wilson carried the region by 11 points, easily the strongest result for the Democrats up to that point in the two-party era, and he also performed better in Cuyahoga County than any Democrat in that same time frame. His timing was good, because Greater Cleveland was becoming more electorally important than ever: Cuyahoga County cast the most presidential votes in the state in 1916, eclipsing Hamilton County as Ohio's biggest vote producer. Cuyahoga continued to cast the most votes in every presidential election into the 21st century. Hamilton voted for Hughes, but Wilson otherwise swept the state's 10 most populous counties, including Cuyahoga, Franklin, Lucas (Toledo), Montgomery (Dayton), Summit (Akron), Stark (Canton), and Mahoning (Youngstown).

"The absolutely critical state in 1916 was Ohio," wrote Wilson biographer John Milton Cooper Jr. "Had Wilson swept the West, including California, he still would have lost if he had not made this one substantial crack in the Republican heartland."[11] Ohio was the only midwestern state that Wilson carried, and it was actually a couple of points more Democratic than the nation.

Wilson had provided Democrats with a blueprint to win Ohio: an alliance of rural counties that had been sympathetic to the South during the Civil War and most of the state's big urban counties, many of which had growing numbers of ethnic voters. But, four years later, that blueprint went up in smoke.

## A RETURN TO NORMALCY, 1920–1924

Almost immediately after Wilson was sworn in for a second term, the nation entered World War I. On November 5, 1918—Wilson's second midterm—the Republicans swept to national victories and captured both the House and the Senate, a not uncommon occurrence for a midterm (the president's party often does poorly, as previously noted). This time, "high prices, wartime shortages, and myriad inconveniences" contributed to the Democrats' woes.[12] One Democratic survivor of the Republican onslaught was the incumbent governor of Ohio, James Cox, a Dayton newspaper publisher.

Six days later, the Central Powers in Europe surrendered. The United States and the Allies had won the war. Wilson's last two years in office were far from peaceful, however. A communist scare gripped the nation amid national strikes, including a bitter steelworker walkout across northeast Ohio in the latter half of 1919. The economy also dipped after the war, always a worrying sign for the incumbent party going into a presidential election.

The 1920 election was a banner moment for the Ohio bellwether: both major parties nominated Buckeyes as their candidates. Senator Warren G. Harding carried the banner for the Republicans and Cox won the Democratic nomination. Not only were both Ohioans, but both were also newspaper men: Cox's paper was the *Dayton Daily News*, while Harding's was the *Marion Star* (Marion County is about an hour north of Columbus).

After voting for Wilson in part because he had promised to keep the nation out of war, Ohio's Germans were not happy that the nation had entered the war anyway. They also harbored a second grievance against the Democrats: amid a flurry of anti-German activity during and after the war, Governor Cox supported a bill, called the Ake Law, forbidding the teaching of German in any school below the eighth grade.[13]

Harding, promising a "Return to Normalcy," romped to victory both nationally and in Ohio in 1920. That Cox actually performed a few points better in Ohio than he did nationally is a testament to Harding's nearly 25-point victory. Harding performed better in heavily German northwest Ohio than any Republican ever had, becoming the first Republican presidential candidate ever to carry counties such as Ottawa (mentioned above as having a large first-generation German population), Defiance, Henry, and Putnam. These were counties that had stuck with the Democrats even in Parker's blowout loss to Roosevelt in 1904, but it's likely that the war and anti-German antagonism pushed some of the German counties out of the incumbent party's camp. The German swing is reflected by the results in some other states, like Wisconsin, that had a larger German population than Ohio: over the last 30 elections, the Badger State's biggest Republican lean compared to the national voting came in 1920.

All told, Harding carried 80 of 88 Ohio counties, including all the major urban ones. Normalcy was restored: after two cycles off the elephant's reservation, Ohio and the nation had returned to the Republican camp.

Ohio's total presidential votes nearly doubled from 1916 to 1920, from about 1.17 million to 2.02 million, thanks to women's suffrage. Still, it's hard to discern any major change in the state's political leanings from this influx of new voters. The so-called gender gap in American politics—women being more Democratic and men being more Republican—didn't manifest itself nationally until around 1980.[14]

Harding died in office in 1923. In the 90 years prior to his death, an Ohioan had lived in the White House for 27 of them. In the 90-plus years since, none has called the mansion home for even a day.

Vice President Calvin Coolidge took over, and in 1924 the Republicans chose him as their nominee at the convention in Cleveland. (Charles Dawes, who was from Illinois but was born in Marietta, was his running mate.) Coolidge easily carried the state and won the election, but he lost in the city where he had been nominated. Senator Robert LaFollette, a Wisconsin Republican running under the Progressive Party banner, launched a third-party bid, winning close to 17 percent nationally. Coolidge cruised with 54 percent of the total vote, while hapless Democrat John W. Davis won only 29 percent. LaFollette had been nominated in a Cleveland convention as well, and he actually carried the city (though not Cuyahoga County as a whole), thanks in part to the support of rising star journalist Louis Seltzer of the *Cleveland Press*, who later served as the paper's editor for more than three decades. Overall, northeast Ohio gave about one of every four of its presidential votes to LaFollette in 1924, echoing its support for Roosevelt's Progressive bid a dozen years before. Davis, like Cox four years earlier, carried only eight small counties.

## The Democrats' Urban Turn, 1928–1932

The West Virginian John W. Davis, "a man whose law firm served J. P. Morgan and other financial interests,"[15] was hardly a progressive Democrat, and in 1928 the party turned to a different kind of nominee: New York Governor Al Smith, a Catholic and a "Wet" (meaning that he opposed Prohibition, which had been instituted nationally in 1920). Smith became the third straight Democrat to lose nationally, and lose Ohio in a wipeout—this time, to Republican Herbert Hoover—but hidden in the numbers were some telling signs for the future.

Throughout the early 20th century, immigration from Europe to Ohio had continued in earnest, but the new arrivals were no longer chiefly of German and Irish descent. Czechoslovakians, Hungarians, Italians, Poles, and many other groups arrived in significant numbers.

In the 1930 census, about 10 percent of the state's residents were foreign-born whites, and they lived disproportionately in northeast Ohio, attracted by factory jobs in that region's booming industrial sectors. Of about 650,000 foreign-born white Ohioans, more than 40 percent lived just in Cuyahoga County. By comparison, less than 10 percent lived in Franklin and Hamilton Counties *combined.* All told, more than three in five Cuyahoga County residents had been born in another country or had at least one foreign-born parent. Several other northeast Ohio counties had a similar profile, while most of the rest of the state had far smaller percentages of immigrants or children of immigrants. Some exceptions were Lucas County (Toledo) as well as Belmont and Jefferson Counties along the Ohio River in the southeast. Immigrants likely gravitated to all three because of work in heavy industry and coal, respectively.

According to Kevin Phillips, by nominating Smith, a Catholic candidate who appealed to ethnics and urbanites, "the Democrats were giving the foreign-stock, usually-Catholic city dweller a party with which he could identify."[16] The political journalist Michael Barone added that Smith "ran far better than previous Democrats in Catholic immigrant areas in the Northeast and Great Lakes."[17] Although Smith carried only two Ohio counties—Mercer and Putnam in the state's northwestern quadrant, both of which were and are heavily Catholic—he did perform well in some ethnic, industrial counties like Cuyahoga, where he ran five points better than he did nationally.

Still, anti-Catholic sentiment doomed him across the state, including in cities like Akron and Youngstown, which had a significant Ku Klux Klan presence. In fact, several local officials in Summit County (Akron), were reputedly Klan members in the mid-1920s. The KKK hates, among many other groups, Catholics. Smith was crushed in other parts of the state, too, as in Amish Holmes County and its neighbors, Ashland and Wayne. Prior to 1928, all three consistently leaned to the Democrats; this time, they were notably more Republican than the state as a whole. Major swings in presidential deviation toward the Republicans were common across the state that year. It's worth noting that the Klan was hardly confined to northeast Ohio: the KKK claimed 400,000 members statewide,[18] and its influence was crucial in pushing the state legislature to pass a bill in 1925 requiring the reading of the Bible in public schools. One of those opposing this bill was a young Republican state representative from Hamilton County and the son of a former president: Robert A. Taft, who argued in vain that the bill violated the Constitution and would be "a calamity if it were to pass."[19] The governor vetoed the bill, and the Klan's influence thereafter began to wane.

Hoover's triumph was short-lived, however: The Great Depression began less than a year after his election, and the economic calamity doomed his chances for a second term. Democrats chose Franklin D. Roosevelt, Smith's successor as New York governor and Cox's running mate from 1920. History might have turned out differently if the Democrats had instead opted for former Cleveland mayor and Wilson administration Secretary of War Newton D. Baker. Had FDR's opponents succeeded in stopping him at the convention, it's possible that Baker, a conservative Democrat and West Virginia native, might have become Ohio's ninth president.[20]

While 1932 ushered in an era of 20 straight years of Democratic control of the White House, it was in some ways the end of an era, not the beginning of one. That's because FDR used an old playbook to win Ohio the first time. "FDR won by a small but clear margin an election which . . . was striking because of the restoration of the pre–World War I pattern,"[21] wrote Ohio political historian Thomas Flinn. In other words, Roosevelt's areas of strength in Ohio were similar to those of other post–Civil War Democrats. Roosevelt performed best in the northwest, while only barely winning the other regions of the state.

The 12 counties that gave FDR more than 60 percent of the two-party vote in 1932 generally had small populations, and all of them had voted for McClellan over Lincoln in 1864. Meanwhile, Roosevelt underperformed in Cuyahoga County and didn't even win Mahoning County (Youngstown), two counties that soon would become among the most Democratic in the state. But not quite yet: Wilson, in 1916, did better in both counties than Roosevelt did in his first election. Overall, FDR won Ohio by less than three points, while he won by 18 nationally. Despite changing demographics, residual partisan loyalties limited FDR's performance in the Buckeye State.

And there was another factor. The state's black population was growing, and, as of 1932, it remained heavily Republican.

By 1930, Ohio's population was 4.6 percent black—still a small percentage, but nearly double what it had been in 1890. By 1970, the percentage of black residents had doubled again, to 9.1 percent, as more and more blacks left the South. Black voters remained loyal to the Party of Lincoln through the early part of the 20th century, and in Ohio they voted overwhelmingly for Hoover. According to Nancy J. Weiss in *Farewell to the Party of Lincoln*, black precincts in Cleveland and Cincinnati voted 82 percent to 17 percent and 71 percent to 29 percent, respectively, for Hoover.[22] More than two-fifths of all of Ohio's black residents lived in those two counties at that time, so their votes clearly limited FDR's performance (even though he won both counties).

All told, Ohio was eight points more Republican than the nation in 1932—its biggest deviation in either direction from the national two-party vote between 1896 and 2012. Ohio was through with Hoover, but its message to Roosevelt was not one of affirmation. The only states where Roosevelt did worse than Ohio were confined to the Northeast and Middle Atlantic: he lost four of six New England states and two others, Delaware and Pennsylvania. Connecticut voted for Hoover, but only by a point; northeast Ohio hewed closely to its Connecticut "motherland," going for Roosevelt, but only by a few hundredths of a point.

The Roosevelt Revolution had to wait another four years in Ohio. But when it arrived in 1936, the state's political geography changed in a way that would endure for decades to come.

# FIVE

## *Roosevelt, Eisenhower,*

## *and Nixon—but Not Taft, 1936–1972*

Although Ohio voted for Franklin Roosevelt in 1932, the state's real political transformation did not come until 1936, as Roosevelt's tremendously popular New Deal programs won him the loyalty of the nation's downscale voters, "drawing to [him] enormous majorities in the working-class industrial cities," as David Kennedy wrote in *Freedom from Fear*.[1]

Roosevelt's massive margins in counties with heavily ethnic industrial centers locked in Democratic voting patterns that persist to this day. Mahoning County (Youngstown) swung from giving just 44 percent of its vote to FDR in 1932 to 71 percent in 1936; Cuyahoga County (Cleveland) moved from 50 percent to 65 percent. Before 1936, it had been common for both counties to vote more Republican than the state. After 1936, they always leaned strongly Democratic compared to the rest of the state.

Jefferson County (Steubenville), the Ohio River mining and industrial county mentioned in chapter 4 as having an above-average immigrant population at this time, also generally had leaned Republican before 1936. After 1936, it leaned reliably Democratic for the rest of the century. Roosevelt also substantially improved his performance in Summit County (Akron), Cuyahoga's industrial neighbor to the south. It, too, never looked back, along with Trumbull County, home to Warren, which at that time was a steel center just like Youngstown.

Particularly in the northeast—the old Connecticut Western Reserve—the 1936 election locked in a strong Democratic identity that largely endures to this day. So much for a comeback for Republicans in Cleveland, where in 1936 they nominated landslide loser Alf Landon, the governor of Kansas. It was the last major party nominating convention held in the state until the Republicans again met in Cleveland in July 2016.

Additionally, Ohio black voters who previously had been suspicious of FDR strongly supported his reelection. After losing handily among African Americans in Cleveland and Cincinnati in 1932, FDR won 61 percent and 65 percent in black-dominated districts in those cities, respectively, four years later, according to Nancy Weiss's research.[2] Black voters nationally and in Ohio "responded to the New Deal on economic grounds." One woman in Columbus wrote to Roosevelt, "Me and my people have been able to live through the depression with food shoes clothing and fuel all through the kindheartness [*sic*] thoughtfulness and sane leadership of Roosevelt." Democrats did not act on African Americans' civil rights priorities until after FDR had left the scene, but his programs helped them in their time of need—and that was more than the GOP, the historic party of black voters, was doing for them.[3]

At the same time, some rural parts of the state to which the old, more conservative Democratic Party had appealed saw their old loyalties tested. In these counties, places with few black voters and low percentages of recent immigrants, the Democrats' liberal turn was unwelcome.

All told, 17 counties that had been more Democratic than the state overall in 1932 became more Republican than the state in 1936—and then never again had a Democratic-leaning presidential deviation into the 21st century. Five others became more Republican in 1936, and, with just one or two exceptions, have stayed that way since. All told, a quarter of the state's 88 counties locked in Republican-leaning voting patterns that remained in place at least through 2012.[4] These counties together cast only 12 percent of Ohio's two-party votes in 1936, so they did not represent a large absolute number of votes—Cuyahoga alone cast 15 percent of the state's votes in that election—but these places were never friendly to Democrats again.

Michael Barone, writing in *Our Country*, made two separate observations that help put the Ohio changes in context. On one hand, in almost all major industrial areas, "party preference based on ethnic tradition was replaced in the cities by an all but uniform preference for the Democrats." On the other hand, however, "in a majority of the nation's 3,000-plus counties, Roosevelt's percentage went down, not up."[5] The tradeoff was a positive one for Democrats in Ohio and across most of the nation in 1936 as FDR improved his performance from 1932. The voting shifts pushed Ohio's presidential deviation from R +8 in 1932 to R +2 in 1936, realigning the state's voting pattern to hew more closely to the national average after having leaned to the Republicans in the previous three elections.

Just eight years later, however—for the first time in nearly half a century—Ohio would pick a loser in the presidential race. The changes that FDR had made to the state's electorate would endure, but his big majorities would not.

### THE YEARS OF BRICKER AND TAFT, 1940–1952

Two years after FDR's towering triumph, a faltering economy and the president's own overreach—most notably on a failed plan to expand the Supreme Court in order to create a high judiciary friendlier to the New Deal—led to an epic midterm shellacking in 1938.

The Democrats lost 71 House seats and six Senate seats, including the one held by Democrat Robert J. Bulkley, who was elected to his first full term in 1932 in a much more Democratic-leaning election. The man who a decade earlier had questioned mandatory Bible reading in Ohio schools, Republican Robert A. Taft, was headed to the US Senate. Taft's fellow Republican, John W. Bricker, won the Ohio governor's mansion. Neither would ever be part of a winning national presidential ticket, but both played critical roles in the national GOP for parts of the next two decades.

Taft and Bricker performed almost identically statewide (53.6 percent and 52.5 percent, respectively), confining Democratic support to the big, industrial, ethnic counties of Cuyahoga, Mahoning, and Summit, as well as a handful of other counties, like Belmont and Jefferson along the Ohio River. Even in a midterm year, the ancestrally strong rural Democratic counties of the northwestern and western parts of the state were quickly abandoning them.

In 1940, Taft sought the Republican presidential nomination. Bricker, the other rising Ohioan, had announced in mid-1939 that he would not run. In the months leading up to the convention, the freshman senator assumed that his main opponent would be Thomas Dewey, the young Republican governor of New York.

Taft "had two handicaps that pulled him back" in 1940, though, wrote biographer James T. Patterson. The first was his cold speaking style. "Taft speaks as if he were submitting a brief in a probate case rather than addressing an audience which might number several million fellow citizens," one of his staffers observed. The second was the storm of war in Europe. On May 10, Nazi dictator Adolf Hitler's armies smashed into France and the Low Countries, and by June 22 the French had surrendered to the Germans. Two days later, the Republican convention opened in Philadelphia, and a dark horse candidate, utilities executive Wendell Willkie, garnered the nomination.[6]

In the 2010s, outsider Tea Party Republicans frequently complained about the party establishment's lack of conservatism and, to them, weak choices of candidates, but their complaints were nothing new. The insider-versus-outsider battle that has often defined the Republican Party dates back to at least the election of 1940, when internationalist elites got their man, Willkie, the nomination over the midwesterner Taft, a critic of American intervention in Europe. "You may or may not become President," former vice president Charles G. Dawes told Taft after Willkie won the nomination, "but the important thing is that you deserve to be."[7]

Roosevelt ran for an unprecedented third term, easily dispatching Willkie by 10 points nationally. That margin was closer than those of FDR's first two victories, though, and as the journalist Samuel Lubell pointed out in an election postmortem, "it was no great victory." This was an era accustomed to blowouts, however, and Roosevelt's share of the vote was the lowest of any presidential winner since Wilson's narrow 1916 victory. Lubell called it the first "class-conscious vote" in American history, with labor, African Americans, and "the foreign born and their first and second generation descendants" powering FDR to victory.[8]

Roosevelt's margin in Ohio was smaller, 52 percent to 48 percent, with his best performance coming in the industrial northeast, where he won 58 percent. The city of Cleveland won the region and the state for FDR.

Lubell noted that Roosevelt won the city by 150,000 votes, about the same as his statewide plurality: the rest of the state outside Cleveland's borders was basically a draw. Without Cleveland's dramatic turn toward the Democrats, Ohio would have been considerably more Republican than the nation, just as it had been in FDR's first election.

The northwest was FDR's worst Ohio region, after having been his best just eight years earlier. As in 1920, it's likely that a Democratic president's seeming hostility toward Germany upset voters in some of these heavily German counties. In 1936, some of these northwestern counties had given substantial percentages, 10 to 20 percent of the vote, to isolationist Union Party presidential candidate William Lemke, a proxy for Father Charles Coughlin, an influential crypto-fascist and anti-Semitic Catholic radio priest based in Detroit. His message found an attentive audience among at least some voters in heavily Catholic northwest Ohio. Phillips interpreted the Lemke vote in Ohio and other places as a precursor to the sharp turn many German Catholics took against Roosevelt in 1940.

That German Americans turned against Roosevelt on foreign policy grounds is not a universal view. Bernard Sternsher, for instance, argued that German Americans in Northwest Ohio would have moved toward the Republicans in 1940 even without World War II. According to Sternsher, these were and are conservative areas that had "an adverse reaction to the New Deal." Given the rural-urban split that later came to define American politics—the big cities Democratic and the rural areas Republican—Sternsher may have had a point.[9]

Taft's Hamilton County narrowly voted for Willkie, starting a long period during which Cincinnati and its closest suburbs became one of the greatest areas of Republican urban strength in the whole country. In fact, Cincinnati was the only large US city that Roosevelt did not carry.[10] Hamilton County backed Democrat Lyndon Johnson in his 1964 landslide, but otherwise uniformly voted Republican from 1940 through 2004. One big difference between Democratic-leaning Cuyahoga and Republican-leaning Hamilton is that, in the 1940 census, Cuyahoga had seven times the number of foreign-born whites as Hamilton.

Four years later, Roosevelt again ran for reelection, this time in the middle of World War II. Taft, who faced reelection to the Senate in 1944, demurred, opening the way for fellow Ohioan Bricker to seek the GOP nomination. Bricker was "much more charismatic than Taft and far less thoughtful and sophisticated," wrote historian Andrew Cayton in *Ohio: The History of a People.*[11] Democrat Stephen M. Young, who defeated then Senator Bricker in a 1958 upset, called him "the white-haired darling of the reactionaries,"[12] an assessment that paled in comparison to the opinion of journalist John Gunther, who said of Bricker: "Intellectually he is like interstellar space—a vast vacuum occasionally crossed by homeless, wandering clichés."[13] There are reasons why Taft is remembered as more of a 20th-century intellectual titan than Bricker.

Bricker failed in his bid for the presidency, losing out to Dewey but becoming the New Yorker's running mate. Bricker's vice-presidential candidacy holds a somewhat dubious distinction in a state known as an electoral powerhouse: he was the last Ohioan as of 2012 to appear on a major party presidential ticket, a dry spell older than the oldest of the postwar Baby Boomers.

It is a blemish on Ohio's presidential voting record that in FDR's fourth election, conducted during World War II, which the United States had entered in December 1941, the Buckeye State actually voted against the presidential winner. Bricker's presence on the ticket is a possible and even likely explanation for the bellwether's errancy, though it's hard to prove definitively.

FDR won 55.0 percent of the 1940 two-party vote, but he took only 52.2 percent in Ohio that year. In 1944, FDR's national two-party plurality fell again, to 53.8 percent. This 1.2-point swing away from FDR nationally—assuming a uniform swing across all states—suggests that Roosevelt's share in Ohio should have declined from 52.2 percent to 51.0 percent, still good enough to win.

But there was no tidy, uniform swing that year: Roosevelt's two-party share did not decline by exactly 1.2 points in any state, and in Ohio it fell by 2.4 points, leaving FDR at 49.8 percent and giving the Dewey-Bricker ticket a narrow victory. Could that extra 1.2 points of swing away from the president in Ohio be explained by a hometown effect for Bricker? It could be, although more than a third of all states swung more than 2.4 points away from Roosevelt in 1944, so Ohio's larger-than-average swing was hardly out of the ordinary.

However, there are explanations for the bigger Republican shifts in some of the other states. For instance, 1944 was the last year in which all 11 states of the old Confederacy—the Democratic Solid South—voted together for a Democratic presidential candidate, a pattern that these states had followed with few exceptions since 1880. Of the 17 states in which FDR's two-party vote declined by more than in Ohio from 1940 to 1944, eight were Solid South states, and a ninth, Kentucky, is arguably a southern state too. The South's move toward the Republicans had begun. Several of these other states—Arizona, Idaho, Kansas, and Wyoming—became and remained among the most Republican states in the Union in the second half of the 20th century. Ohio was not on a similar trajectory. In fact, it was not as Republican compared to the nation as it was in 1944 (R +4 presidential deviation) in any subsequent election through 2012.

If one sets those states aside, Ohio's increased Republican tilt in 1944 becomes more noteworthy, especially because the Buckeye State showed the biggest drop for FDR in the Midwest. So perhaps Bricker's vice-presidential candidacy was the decisive factor, but it's hard to say for sure. Political scientists generally don't think running mates have much of an effect on election results. John Sides wrote, "There's just not much evidence that running mates help or hurt that much,"[14] and one study found that from 1884 to 1984, a presidential ticket did only 0.3 points better than expected in the running mate's home state.[15] Such a small swing wouldn't have been enough to push Ohio from red to blue in 1944. Another analysis, however, by election forecaster Nate Silver, suggested that running mates are worth, on average, 2.2 points to the ticket and that Bricker's impact in 1944 was also 2.2 points.[16] So, by Silver's calculation, Bricker did make the difference. Bricker won five statewide elections from 1938 to 1952 (six, if one includes the 1944 presidential result), so it makes sense that he could have been worth a point or two.

But there was yet another important factor in 1944: many Ohioans were fighting overseas. About 12 percent of Ohio's population served in the military,[17] and voting-age personnel participated at a rate of only 28 percent in 1944, just half that of the overall population, according to Donald Inbody's *The Soldier Vote*.[18] The number of raw votes cast nationally declined in 1944 from 1940's level, mostly hurting Roosevelt: he received about 1.7 million fewer votes, while Dewey received about 330,000 fewer votes than Willkie had four years earlier. The same was true in Ohio, but the drop-off for the incumbent was even starker. Dewey came very close to matching Willkie's total, falling just 4,480 votes short, while FDR lost 162,376 votes, a major factor in a statewide election that he lost by only 11,530 votes.

While we do not know exactly how soldiers voted, preelection polling by George Gallup found that younger voters and members of the military—two groups that overlapped—were more Democratic than typical voters. It seems clear that FDR lost votes because of mobilization and that Republicans, for partisan reasons, worked together with southern Democrats, who were trying to prevent mobilized blacks from voting, to stifle efforts to make it easier for soldiers to vote, according to Ira Katznelson in *Fear Itself*.[19] If soldiers had voted at or close to the rate of the regular electorate, FDR almost certainly would have won Ohio, Bricker notwithstanding.

In any event, Ohio had voted for the losing presidential candidate for the first time since 1892. Although the state was consistently more Republican than the nation throughout this period, an odd confluence of events pushed it away from the winner that year.

Taft won a narrow reelection in 1944, and Bricker joined Taft in the US Senate in 1946. Democrat Harry Truman was now president, having taken over after Roosevelt died just a few months into his fourth term.

Taft again tried for the Republican nomination in 1948, but lost it to Dewey. The eastern wing of the GOP, the Willkie-Dewey wing, had triumphed over the midwesterner once again. After conceding to Dewey, Taft told reporters that his second bid for the presidency would be his last. "Like everyone else, he expected Dewey to hold it for eight years."[20]

Gallup's final approval rating poll on Truman, taken in late June, showed him at a weak 40 percent. Former Roosevelt advisor-turned-conservative commentator Raymond Moley, an Ohio native, wrote a few days before the election, "It is easy to predict the election of Governor Dewey. . . . There can be no doubt about the outcome."[21] Moley was not alone: Dewey went into the election a clear favorite. Yet Truman would shock the experts, winning by four points nationally and by about a quarter of a point in Ohio, the smallest margin of victory for any Ohio winner from 1896 to 2012. What happened?

## 1948 Ohio Presidential Election

| | | | |
|---|---|---|---|
| Dewey (R) | 1,445,684 | 49.24% |
| *Truman (D) | 1,452,791 | 49.48% |
| Other | 37,596 | 1.28% |
| Variance (D) | 7,107 | 0.24% |

**West Region**

| | | |
|---|---|---|
| Republican | 175,519 | 49.70% |
| Democrat | 175,648 | 49.74% |
| Other | 1,968 | 0.56% |
| Variance (D) | 129 | 0.04% |

**Northwest Region**

| | | |
|---|---|---|
| Republican | 153,466 | 52.82% |
| Democrat | 134,613 | 46.33% |
| Other | 2,463 | 0.85% |
| Variance (R) | 18,853 | 6.49% |

**Northeast Region**

| | | |
|---|---|---|
| Republican | 556,824 | 45.91% |
| Democrat | 629,288 | 51.89% |
| Other | 26,694 | 2.20% |
| Variance (D) | 72,464 | 5.98% |

**Southwest Region**

| | | |
|---|---|---|
| Republican | 210,516 | 51.91% |
| Democrat | 192,449 | 47.45% |
| Other | 2,581 | 0.64% |
| Variance (R) | 18,067 | 4.46% |

**Central Region**

| | | |
|---|---|---|
| Republican | 240,336 | 54.18% |
| Democrat | 201,034 | 45.32% |
| Other | 2,188 | 0.49% |
| Variance (R) | 39,302 | 8.86% |

**Southeast Region**

| | | |
|---|---|---|
| Republican | 109,023 | 47.30% |
| Democrat | 119,759 | 51.96% |
| Other | 1,702 | 0.74% |
| Variance (D) | 10,736 | 4.66% |

MAP 5.1. The 1948 presidential election in Ohio. *Source:* OhioElectionResults.com

Truman's map of victory in Ohio looks like nothing that came before it or after it, a mishmash of counties in all corners of the state. Truman bled a considerable amount of support to Dewey in the industrial northeast, winning just 53 percent in Cuyahoga County, where Roosevelt had won 60 percent four years earlier. Henry Wallace, FDR's vice president from 1941 to 1945, ran as a progressive third-party candidate in 1948 and scored 3.6 percent of the vote in Cuyahoga, probably hurting Truman more than Dewey. But Truman made up for his relative weakness in northeast Ohio by reviving, to some degree, the old rural Democratic coalition in other parts of the state.

Ancestrally Democratic, German Catholic counties like Mercer and Putnam swung back to Truman after abandoning Roosevelt, in part over war-related grievances, in 1940 and 1944. "In six largely German-American counties in western Ohio alone," Lubell wrote in *The Future of American Politics*, "Truman picked up more than 6,700 votes over Roosevelt's 1944 showing, while the Republican lost 13,000 votes."[22] In 1936, Father Coughlin's cat's-paw William Lemke carried 21 precincts in Ohio. Eleven of these switched from Dewey in 1944 to Truman in 1948. "Throughout the country," Lubell wrote, "one finds a remarkable parallel between Truman's gains and the vote given Coughlin's Union party in 1936."[23] One explanation, identified by Patterson and others, was "falling farm prices, which Truman shrewdly if unfairly blamed" on the Republican-controlled Congress.[24] But the farm country revival was short-lived, and the Democratic vote was becoming more concentrated. For instance, 37 of Ohio's 88 counties voted more Democratic than the state as a whole in 1916. In 1948, just 21 counties voted more Democratic than the statewide average. Even in an election in which Truman showed some improvement from Roosevelt's 1940 and 1944 efforts in rural areas, the industrial northeast was still critical to his victory.

The GOP had another strong midterm in 1950, which coincided with the beginning of the Korean War, and Taft dispatched his opponent, Ohio state auditor "Jumping Joe" Ferguson, with ease. Ferguson was unsophisticated, to say the least: When asked about Quemoy and Matsu, islands held by Chinese nationalists that were under attack by mainland communists, Ferguson said that he would "carry them both in this election."[25] Ferguson's foreign policy, he said, was "Beat Michigan," in reference to the Ohio State football team's northern rival.[26] Taft blew open what many expected to be a close election, prompting Lubell to ask, "Does [Taft's] 430,000 majority in a state Truman won by only 7,107 votes in 1948 presage a Republican presidential victory in 1952, with Taft perhaps the GOP standard bearer?"[27]

The answer ended up being yes to the first question and no to the second. Taft ran for a third time in 1952, coming closer than he previously had to gaining the GOP nomination. He actually entered the convention with more delegates than General Dwight Eisenhower, a nominal Republican whom the eastern establishment had drafted into the party to stop its long presidential drought. Taft also won more primary votes, although the primaries were not nearly as meaningful then as they became later in the century. Eisenhower performed well in the few places he was on the ballot, defeating Taft in the lead-off contest in New Hampshire. "Both sides maneuvered shrewdly" at the July convention, wrote Clarence E. Wunderlin Jr. in his compilation of Taft's correspondence, but Ike got the nomination.[28]

Taft, ultimately, was never enough of an internationalist to win the party's nomination. Henry Luce, the powerful publisher of *Time*, pushed Eisenhower's candidacy aggressively. Luce and Taft found themselves on opposite sides of several foreign policy issues going back to before the United States' entry into World War II. In a May 1941 national radio address, Taft had accused Luce and his allies of "seem[ing] to contemplate an Anglo-American alliance perpetually ruling the world. Frankly, the American people don't want to rule the world, and we are not equipped to do it."[29] Luce and his media empire were frequent critics of Taft and helped prevent him from ever winning the nomination. In an analysis of the convention results, published posthumously by the conservative magazine *Human Events*, Taft blamed the eastern establishment and the press: "Four-fifths of the influential newspapers in the country were opposed to me continuously and vociferously and many turned themselves into propaganda sheets for my opponent."[30]

Years later, Luce asked a liberal friend why Taft (who had died in 1953, only months after becoming Senate majority leader) deserved a monument near the Capitol, a bell tower. According to David Halberstam in *The Powers That Be*, the friend replied: "Don't you know that's the Clarion Tower of Expiation? It's a way of getting rid of the guilt from 1952."[31] Taft's carillon is located just a few hundred feet north of the Capitol, a consolation for the Ohioan who came closest to winning the presidency since Warren Harding in 1920.

Eisenhower, exactly the kind of nationally popular and nonideological candidate the Republicans needed to break what seemed like a Democratic lock on the White House, crushed his Democratic opponent, Illinois Governor Adlai Stevenson, 55 percent to 45 percent. Ike did about a point better in Ohio, carrying 82 of 88 counties, including Cuyahoga (narrowly). Stevenson retained a few strongly Democratic counties along the state's eastern border, like Mahoning and Jefferson, as well as Summit. Eisenhower won more than 60 percent in the northwestern and western parts of the state, showing that Truman's 1948 performance—he narrowly won the western counties and was competitive in the northwest—was just a pit stop on both regions' roads to steady Republicanism.

## Nixon Country, 1952–1972

In February 1981, former president Richard M. Nixon made one of his first public appearances after resigning nearly seven years earlier because of the Watergate scandal. After being introduced by former Ohio State football coach Woody Hayes—who, like Nixon, had lost his job in disgrace (the Buckeye coach had been fired for punching an opposing player during a 1978 bowl game)—Nixon thanked Ohioans for their unwavering support. "I feel I have a very special relationship with [Ohio] from a political standpoint," Nixon said. He added that, of the nation's 10 most populous states, "Ohio is the only one besides my home state of California in which I've never lost a national election, and I thank you for that."[32]

Nixon appeared on five national tickets: in 1952 and 1956 as Eisenhower's running mate and then as the Republican nominee in 1960, 1968, and 1972. Ohio supported those tickets all five times, even though Nixon narrowly lost nationally in 1960.

While Nixon was not an Ohioan, his father had been born in Appalachia, in Vinton County, the state's least populous. Whether Nixon's Ohio roots boosted his record in the state is hard to discern, although he did mention them when campaigning there. Speaking in Athens County (next door to Vinton) late in the 1960 campaign, Nixon noted that he had "a special reason that I have been looking forward to this meeting. . . . It happens that this is the home congressional district of my father."[33]

The Eisenhower-Nixon ticket easily won reelection in 1956, again over Stevenson, 58 percent to 42 percent nationally in the two-party vote and an even better 61 percent to 39 percent in Ohio. The individual counties voted in much the same way as they had four years earlier, but Eisenhower's improved statewide performance won him every county but one, the sparsely populated and historically Democratic Pike County in the south-central part of the state.

Nixon got his chance at the presidency in 1960 against Senator John F. Kennedy, a Massachusetts Democrat who was only the second Catholic to ever be nominated on a major-party ticket—Al Smith in 1928 had been the first. JFK won the national popular vote by just a few tenths of a percentage point, and narrow victories in Illinois and Texas delivered him the presidency. Ohio, meanwhile, backed Nixon, picking the loser for just the second time since 1896. And Ohio really was not that close: Nixon won it 53 percent to 47 percent in the two-party vote, making the state a little more than three points more Republican than the rest of the country.

Kennedy's Catholicism clearly colored the election. According to Gallup, 78 percent of Catholics voted for Kennedy, while 62 percent of Protestants voted for Nixon.[34] In a 1962 analysis, Ohio elections expert Thomas Flinn investigated how Nixon had carried the state, and he argued that the religious factor loomed large. He found that Kennedy's improvement over Stevenson's performance in 1956—JFK did eight points better in the two-party vote, 47 percent versus 39 percent—was attributable almost entirely to gains among Catholics. According to Flinn's calculations, Kennedy made at most only a tiny gain among Ohio's Protestants, 1 percent or so, while he improved dramatically among Catholics. A postelection Gallup analysis found similar results nationally, noting that across the nation Kennedy had barely gained among Protestants but that he had done 28 points better among Catholics. That squares with Flinn's Ohio-level calculations.[35]

Kennedy won only 10 of 88 counties, unsurprisingly concentrated in the northeast and in the typically Democratic Ohio River counties of Belmont and Jefferson, along with Lucas County (Toledo), which was becoming one of the most Democratic counties in Ohio. But a few counties in Kennedy's meager total seemed out of place. For instance, Kennedy became

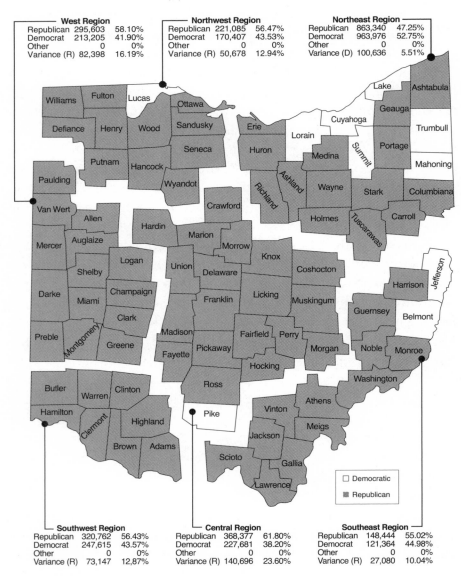

**1960 Ohio Presidential Election**

| | | |
|---|---|---|
| *Nixon (R) | 2,217,611 | 53.28% |
| Kennedy (D) | 1,944,248 | 46.72% |
| Other | 0 | 0% |
| Variance (R) | 273,363 | 6.57% |

**West Region**

| | | |
|---|---|---|
| Republican | 295,603 | 58.10% |
| Democrat | 213,205 | 41.90% |
| Other | 0 | 0% |
| Variance (R) | 82,398 | 16.19% |

**Northwest Region**

| | | |
|---|---|---|
| Republican | 221,085 | 56.47% |
| Democrat | 170,407 | 43.53% |
| Other | 0 | 0% |
| Variance (R) | 50,678 | 12.94% |

**Northeast Region**

| | | |
|---|---|---|
| Republican | 863,340 | 47.25% |
| Democrat | 963,976 | 52.75% |
| Other | 0 | 0% |
| Variance (D) | 100,636 | 5.51% |

**Southwest Region**

| | | |
|---|---|---|
| Republican | 320,762 | 56.43% |
| Democrat | 247,615 | 43.57% |
| Other | 0 | 0% |
| Variance (R) | 73,147 | 12.87% |

**Central Region**

| | | |
|---|---|---|
| Republican | 368,377 | 61.80% |
| Democrat | 227,681 | 38.20% |
| Other | 0 | 0% |
| Variance (R) | 140,696 | 23.60% |

**Southeast Region**

| | | |
|---|---|---|
| Republican | 148,444 | 55.02% |
| Democrat | 121,364 | 44.98% |
| Other | 0 | 0% |
| Variance (R) | 27,080 | 10.04% |

☐ Democratic
▨ Republican

MAP 5.2. The 1960 presidential election in Ohio. *Source:* OhioElectionResults.com

just the second Democrat since the Civil War—FDR in his 1936 landslide was the other—to carry Cuyahoga County's northeastern neighbor, Lake County. Lake is very Catholic. At 35.2 percent, it is the state's third-most Catholic county according to the 2010 US Religious Census, behind only Mercer and Putnam, which were majority Catholic into the 2010s and were the only two Ohio counties that Kennedy's coreligionist Al Smith carried in 1928. Kennedy lost those western counties in 1960, but nowhere in the state did he more improve the Democratic share of the vote from four years earlier: JFK did 17.3 points better than Stevenson in Putnam and 18.9 points better in Mercer (he lost the latter by just five votes).

According to the 1936 religious census, Ohio was 16 percent Catholic at the time. It's about 18 percent today. Generally speaking, the most Catholic counties in 1960 are still the most Catholic today. There is a strong correlation of 0.79 (1 being a perfect relationship) between Kennedy's county-by-county improvement on Stevenson's vote and the percentage of Catholics living in each county today. Ultimately, though, there just weren't enough Catholics in Ohio to get Kennedy over the finish line.

Hidden in the data from that election are other curiosities that can largely be explained by religious affiliation. While Cuyahoga County had become reliably Democratic by the mid-20th century, the state's second- and third-biggest counties, Hamilton and Franklin, were equally reliably Republican. They also generally voted about the same: for a 10-election stretch between 1936 and 1972, each was on average about four points more Republican than the state as a whole, and in nine of those 10 elections the voting in one closely matched that in the other, differing only by a point or two, if at all. The one exception was 1960, when Hamilton was five points more Democratic than Franklin. A likely explanation: Hamilton is about a quarter Catholic, while Franklin is only about an eighth. Kennedy took note of his poor performance in Franklin County, once quipping, "There is no city in the United States in which I get a warmer welcome and fewer votes than Columbus, Ohio."[36]

The next Catholic to win a major party presidential nomination, John Kerry in 2004, found no bonus in the state's two most Catholic counties, Mercer and Putnam. So the religious distinctions of past generations seemed less meaningful in the 21st century.

In 1960, Governor Michael V. DiSalle, a Toledo Democrat, took the heat for Kennedy's loss in Ohio. Two years later, "Tax Hike Mike," as his detractors called him, lost in a landslide to state auditor James A. Rhodes, a Republican who eventually served four terms. Rhodes, a "jobs and progress" governor who was hardly ideological, had little use for Barry Goldwater, a conservative hero who was on pace to win the 1964 Republican presidential nomination.

Rhodes feared—accurately, it turned out—that the Arizona senator would be a fatal drag on the Senate candidacy of Robert Taft Jr., who was trying to follow in his late father's footsteps to the Senate. The governor and the nonideological state Republican Party chairman Ray Bliss—noted in chapter 3 as a proponent of issueless politics—tried to keep Ohio's delegates neutral entering into the 1964 Republican convention. Rhodes controlled the delegation as a favorite son presidential candidate (in other words, one who would get symbolic support in the first round of convention voting but who was not a serious candidate for the nomination), but he seemed to suggest to reporters before the convention that he would be releasing the delegates to vote as they pleased on the first ballot. At least, that's how they heard it, according to a trio of Ohio political reporters in their biography of Rhodes, *Ohio Colossus*.[37] Goldwater won the nomination on the first ballot, going on to a stupendous national defeat that included a crushing loss in Ohio.

Goldwater's loss was a political stick of dynamite, blasting apart the foundations of the state's Republican Party to reveal the most entrenched GOP bedrock below. Just five counties supported Goldwater: Delaware (Franklin County's northern neighbor), Union (just northeast of Franklin), and three northwestern counties, Allen, Fulton, and Hancock (home of Findlay, which Congress later designated "Flag City, U.S.A."). All have retained strong Republican leanings into the 21st century. Meanwhile, Rhodes's fears that Goldwater's sinking campaign would drag down Taft's Senate candidacy were justified: Goldwater lost the state by more than a million votes, while Taft lost by just a shade under 17,000.

Ohio returned to voting with the presidential winner in 1964, and it has not failed to do so since. The state's presidential deviation also has hewed closely to the national average, never straying by more than two points in any election from 1964 to 2012.

Bliss became national Republican Party chairman after the 1964 debacle. Nixon, who had campaigned vigorously for Goldwater and for successful GOP candidates in the party's strong 1966 midterm, reemerged as a presidential contender in 1968. Rhodes preferred his friend Nelson Rockefeller, the longtime governor of New York and frequent but unsuccessful presidential contender, and he withheld the Ohio delegation's vote on the first ballot. Nixon won anyway.[38] Johnson, weighed down by the raging Vietnam War, stepped aside, and Vice President Hubert Humphrey eventually got the nomination at a chaotic Democratic convention in Chicago.

Adding intrigue to the 1968 election—as if LBJ's surrender, Nixon's return, the Vietnam War, and the assassinations of Martin Luther King Jr. and Democratic presidential contender Robert F. Kennedy were not enough—was the third-party candidacy of George Wallace, the former governor of Alabama and a candidate of white resentment against growing civil rights for African Americans. The Wallace campaign put an emphasis on Ohio, "predicting flatly" in late September to a *Toledo Blade* reporter that Wallace would "carry Ohio . . . by getting somewhere about 55 per cent of the vote."[39] This was before Wallace even officially made it on to the Ohio ballot. Under Ohio law at the time, a new political party, in this case Wallace's American Independent Party, needed to gather a number of signatures equal to 15 percent of the total vote in the previous gubernatorial election, which was about 433,000 signatures (an exceedingly high bar). The Wallace campaign gathered the signatures but did not turn them in before a February deadline. The US Supreme Court, in a 6–3 decision issued just 22 days before the election, declared that the burden for getting access was too high and ordered that Wallace's name be placed on the ballot.[40]

Despite his campaign's boasts, Wallace didn't get even close to 55 percent of the vote in Ohio. He managed to clear that level in only two states: his home state of Alabama and its neighbor, Mississippi. He carried three additional southern states, Arkansas, Georgia, and Louisiana, while performing well in the other states of the old Confederacy.

All told, Ohio came quite close to matching the nation's three-way result: Nixon won 43.4 percent nationally to Humphrey's 42.7 percent, with Wallace at 13.5 percent. Ohio's split was 45.2 to 43.0 to 11.8. The

Humphrey-Nixon results unfolded in a predictable way: Humphrey won the northeast but lost the rest of the state, with the exception of the southeast, where he pulled out a very narrow plurality thanks to the regularly Democratic counties of Belmont and Jefferson.

The state's regions of southern settlement gave Wallace a higher-than-average share of the vote. The eight counties fully contained within the old Virginia Military District—the area between Cincinnati and Dayton to the west and Columbus to the east, extending downward to the state's southern border—gave Wallace 19 percent of its votes, far exceeding his statewide performance.[41] That total does not include Warren County, which is northeast of Hamilton County on the periphery of the old district border and which gave Wallace 25 percent. Wallace's second-best county, Clermont, is another Cincinnati satellite wholly included inside the district. All these counties went for Nixon, suggesting that Wallace hurt Nixon more than he hurt Humphrey, which was almost certainly the case nationally as well.

Wallace's support, however, was not restricted to the state's areas of southern settlement. One of the other counties in which he outperformed his statewide average was Summit (Akron), which, as noted in chapter 4, had a significant KKK presence in the 1920s and had long been a destination for migrants from Border and southern states. Wallace won more than 10 percent in the northeast as a whole. Eight years later, when Wallace was running for the Democratic presidential nomination in 1976, the *New York Times* noted that he had won 20 percent in Cleveland's Fifth Ward, an ethnic-dominated, blue-collar area: "If Hollywood were to invent its version of the classic melting-pot neighborhood as it exists in the blue-collar, industrial America of 1976, it could hardly improve on Cleveland's Fifth Ward."[42] Wallace won an estimated 9 percent of the vote from white, manual workers in the North.[43] Blue-collar voters, like those in northeast Ohio, were still reliably Democratic in this election, but Wallace had eaten into this constituency.

Four years later, Nixon faced a primary challenger: Ohio US Representative John Ashbrook, an early Goldwater supporter whose slogan was "No Left Turns"—a critique of what some conservatives saw as Nixon's insufficient conservatism. Little came of Ashbrook's challenge, and he died in 1982 before he could follow through with a challenge to Democratic Senator Howard Metzenbaum. (Metzenbaum, one of the most liberal major politicians in Ohio history, served three Senate terms from 1976 to 1994.) Ashbrook has remained a hero to Ohio conservatives in the decades after his death.

One of the defining moments of Nixon's first term took place in May 1970 at Portage County's Kent State University, when members of the Ohio National Guard shot at a crowd of college students protesting Nixon's bombing of Cambodia as part of the Vietnam War. Governor Rhodes had dispatched the Guard about 40 times since 1968 in response to unrest,[44] but this time he was locked in a competitive Senate primary with Robert Taft Jr. Rhodes was trailing in the polls by high single digits before the primary. The Kent State shootings took place on Monday, May 4. The primary was the following day, and Rhodes lost by less than a point. Veteran reporter Richard Zimmerman, writing in *Ohio Politics*, argued that Kent State probably helped Rhodes narrow the gap.[45]

The campus unrest came at a time when many college students were gaining a measure of formal political power. In 1971, the states ratified the 26th Amendment, lowering the voting age from 21 to 18. In 1972, the Democrats chose an antiwar presidential nominee, Senator George McGovern of South Dakota, to challenge Nixon. McGovern proved to be a national bust, and Nixon carried 49 states, including Ohio, comfortably. But in that election, thanks to the 26th Amendment and college students' loathing of Nixon, a new, small piece of the state's Democratic coalition emerged.

McGovern would carry only two Ohio counties: Lucas (Toledo), which had become reliably Democratic, and Athens, the home of Ohio University. Prior to the 1960s, Athens had been a reliably Republican-leaning county: from 1856 through 1968, Athens had voted Democratic only three times: twice for FDR in 1936 and 1940 and then for LBJ in 1964. Nixon won the county by about three points in 1968, similar to his statewide plurality.

Outside McGovern's home state of South Dakota, where several counties flipped to him after voting for Nixon in 1968 (even though McGovern lost there anyway), only six counties in the entire country that had voted for Nixon in 1968 flipped to McGovern in 1972. Athens is one of them, along with Washtenaw County, Michigan, home to Ann Arbor and the University of Michigan. Portage, home of Kent State, already leaned slightly Democratic before the shootings, and it had narrowly supported Humphrey in 1968. It became more Democratic relative to the state in 1972, going from D +3 to D +8, but Nixon carried it in 1972. Wood County, home of Bowling Green State University, went from R +8 to an even deviation from 1968 to 1972, which suggests another college-student-motivated Democratic shift after the 26th Amendment.

Portage and Wood were swing counties by the 2010s, and from 1972 on Athens was among the most Democratic of counties in Ohio. Athens gave the Democrats a new anchor in the southeast, just in time for an election in which the region would loom large in an exceedingly close contest.

# Six

## *Obama Rewrites the Carter-Clinton Playbook,*

## *1976–2012*

Emboldened by Richard Nixon's resignation in mid-1974, a strong Democratic midterm that featured former astronaut John Glenn's first election to the Senate in Ohio, and the seeming weakness of unelected incumbent President Gerald Ford, a slew of Democrats pursued the party's presidential nomination in 1976. A surprising nominee emerged: Jimmy Carter, the former one-term governor of Georgia. He would become the first president from the Deep South since the Civil War—Lyndon Johnson, from Texas, is not included because Texas is not part of the Deep South—and his winning path to victory both nationally and in Ohio would look different than those that had come before.

Carter seemed like a sure winner for much of the 1976 general election campaign, but he ended up winning by only two points nationally and capturing fewer than 300 electoral votes (297). Ohio was his closest victory—by just 0.27 points—but he could have won without the state. Wisconsin, which he won by slightly less than two points, provided him his decisive 270th electoral vote. Needless to say, Ford came very close to winning.

The Carter coalition was an unusual one, at least compared with previous elections. He carried all the states of the old Confederacy except for Virginia, and he also won some key northeastern and midwestern states, like Massachusetts, Minnesota, New York, and Pennsylvania. Meanwhile, Ford won every state west of Texas except Hawaii, including the West Coast, which by the 2000s would be reliably Democratic.

The Carter campaign recognized the importance of Ohio, dedicating "more money to [Ohio] per capita than to any other."[1] It was money well spent, given Ohio's close margin, which was the state's second-closest of any election in the 1896–2012 time frame (only 1948, decided by three-hundredths of a point less, was tighter).

Key to Carter's Buckeye victory was his overperformance in southeast Ohio, the Appalachian counties that run along the Ohio River. While the region would only cast about 6 percent of the total two-party votes in 1976—about 238,000 of just over four million cast statewide—Carter would win it 55 percent to 45 percent, or by 23,250 votes. It was, relative to the statewide voting, an unusually strong Democratic performance in the area. Eight years earlier, Humphrey had carried the region, but only by 2,774 votes. If Carter had only matched Humphrey in the southeast in 1976, he would have lost statewide: he won Ohio by only 11,116 votes. Outside southeast Ohio, Ford narrowly won the rest of the state.

Athens, as noted at the end of chapter 5, moved into the Democratic coalition four years before, and it remained there in 1976. Sparsely populated Monroe, located just south of Jefferson on the Ohio River, was really the only consistently Democratic county in the region before the New Deal—its lean toward the Party of Jackson was so old that, prior to the creation of the Republican Party, the GOP's Whig ancestors called the county "Dark Monroe" for their inability to win its votes.[2] Kevin Phillips found that Meigs County, just south of Athens, had the heaviest Republican vote fall-off in the state from 1972 to 1976, and that many other places across the country that swung heavily from 1972 to 1976 were, like Meigs, rural and very white.[3]

Phillips argued that Carter's win could be attributed to a major shift among "Southern and Border state poor whites." Carter's southern heritage, outsider image, and evangelical Christianity—southeast Ohio is Ohio's most evangelical-heavy region—all likely helped his strong southeastern performance. Nearly every southeast Ohio county—and many others that also are defined as Appalachian—was more Democratic in 1976 than in 1948, the other closest 20th-century Ohio election. Belmont and Jefferson, the two typically Democratic counties at the northern end of southeast Ohio, were slightly more Democratic in 1948, but they were still two of Carter's best counties in 1976.

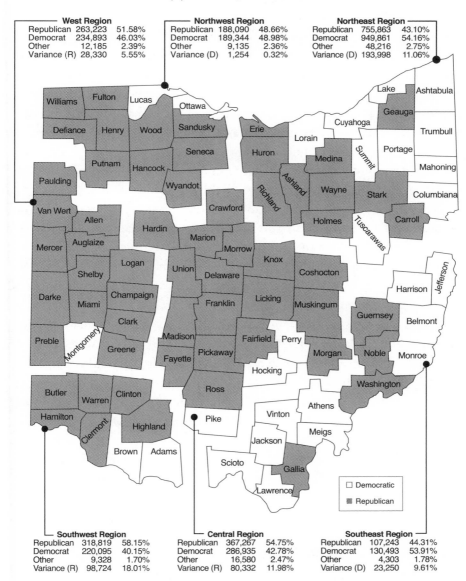

## 1976 Ohio Presidential Election

| | | |
|---|---|---|
| Ford (R) | 2,000,505 | 48.65% |
| *Carter (D) | 2,011,621 | 48.92% |
| Other | 99,747 | 2.43% |
| Variance (D) | 11,116 | 0.27% |

**West Region**

| | | |
|---|---|---|
| Republican | 263,223 | 51.58% |
| Democrat | 234,893 | 46.03% |
| Other | 12,185 | 2.39% |
| Variance (R) | 28,330 | 5.55% |

**Northwest Region**

| | | |
|---|---|---|
| Republican | 188,090 | 48.66% |
| Democrat | 189,344 | 48.98% |
| Other | 9,135 | 2.36% |
| Variance (D) | 1,254 | 0.32% |

**Northeast Region**

| | | |
|---|---|---|
| Republican | 755,863 | 43.10% |
| Democrat | 949,861 | 54.16% |
| Other | 48,216 | 2.75% |
| Variance (D) | 193,998 | 11.06% |

**Southwest Region**

| | | |
|---|---|---|
| Republican | 318,819 | 58.15% |
| Democrat | 220,095 | 40.15% |
| Other | 9,328 | 1.70% |
| Variance (R) | 98,724 | 18.01% |

**Central Region**

| | | |
|---|---|---|
| Republican | 367,267 | 54.75% |
| Democrat | 286,935 | 42.78% |
| Other | 16,580 | 2.47% |
| Variance (R) | 80,332 | 11.98% |

**Southeast Region**

| | | |
|---|---|---|
| Republican | 107,243 | 44.31% |
| Democrat | 130,493 | 53.91% |
| Other | 4,303 | 1.78% |
| Variance (D) | 23,250 | 9.61% |

☐ Democratic
▨ Republican

MAP 6.1. The 1976 presidential election in Ohio. *Source:* OhioElectionResults.com

Carter would win only one White House term. His bid for a second was derailed by stagflation, economic contraction, the Iranian hostage crisis, and the 1980 candidacy of Republican Ronald Reagan.

The story of Reagan's victory in Ohio, which exactly mirrored his victory nationally, is not really one of big shifts in the state's three dominant counties. In 1976, the combined vote total in Cuyahoga, Franklin, and Hamilton Counties produced a 30,091-vote plurality for Ford (Cuyahoga's big Democratic margin was outweighed by a bigger combined GOP edge in Franklin and Hamilton). Four years later, these same counties, combined, produced a 82,316-vote plurality for Reagan. That's obviously a big Republican improvement, and by itself was a turnaround that would have flipped the state given Carter's 11,000-vote win four years prior, but it was only a small portion of Reagan's towering 454,131-vote margin overall. In both elections, the three counties cast about a third of the state's two-party votes.

The big difference was not in the large urban counties, but in the growing "collar counties" around the three major urban counties. Collar counties are the suburban counties that surround a major urban county. The term is most frequently used to describe the counties that encircle Cook County (Chicago), but the term can just as easily be applied to the counties that surround Ohio's most populous counties.

These counties, 15 of them surrounding Cleveland's Cuyahoga, Columbus's Franklin, and Cincinnati's Hamilton,[4] were becoming increasingly important in statewide elections as the state's population started to move to the suburbs and exurbs. In 1948, these 15 counties cast 14 percent of the state's two-party votes, and were basically a tie in that election (Dewey won them by 436 votes out of more than 413,000 cast). Throughout the '50s, '60s, and '70s these counties would continue to reflect the state, deviating at most one or two points from the statewide results in any given election, while continuing to grow as a share of the state's total two-party vote. In 1976, Carter actually won 51 percent of the two-party vote in the collars as they cast about 19 percent of the state's votes.

But the collars swung heavily toward the Republicans in 1980, giving Reagan 58.1 percent of the two-party vote even as he was winning 55.7 percent statewide. Reagan's 126,725-vote plurality in these counties accounted for more than a quarter of his statewide margin. While the collar counties contain some Democratic strongholds—Cuyahoga's southern neighbor, Summit, is included here even as it is the home of Akron, Ohio's fifth most-populous city—this group has been both trending increasingly Republican and growing as a share of the electorate. By the 2000s the collars would be casting a quarter of the state's presidential votes, and they would be leaning about five to six points to the Republicans.

Among the contenders for the right to challenge and ultimately be crushed by Reagan was Ohio Senator John Glenn, a Democrat who in 1984 was in the midst of his second term in the Senate. Despite Glenn's compelling personal story—he was the first American to orbit the Earth, and Carter considered him for vice president in 1976 before picking Mondale—the 1984 presidential nomination became a two-man race between former Vice President Walter Mondale and Senator Gary Hart of Colorado, with Glenn reduced to a nonfactor as voting began. Glenn would serve in the Senate for four terms, retiring in 1998.

Buoyed by tremendous economic growth in the second half of his first term, Reagan easily beat Mondale, the eventual Democratic nominee, 59 percent to 41 percent nationally and by a very similar margin in Ohio. Even Athens, the now reliably Democratic college county, voted for Reagan, and Lucas did for the second election in a row. Mondale actually performed better in a handful of typically Democratic counties than Carter had four years prior, like Cuyahoga and Mahoning, which might have had something to do with Mondale being a more conventional liberal Democratic candidate than the southern evangelical Carter. Also, some of those who supported moderate Republican John Anderson (running in this race as an independent), who won 6 percent statewide in 1980, might have flipped to the Democrats four years later. Still, Reagan's 1984 win was an absolute rout.

Hart, who came close to beating Mondale for the Democratic nomination in 1984, appeared to be a top contender for the 1988 Democratic nomination, but an extramarital affair drove him from the race in 1987 (he would return to the race before the primaries but ended up being a nonfactor). The Hart developments had a domino effect on the race, likely prompting Arkansas Governor Bill Clinton to take a pass on the race because of his own extramarital indiscretions. Another potential Democratic contender was Richard F. Celeste, then in his second term as governor of Ohio. After the Hart story broke, a reporter asked Celeste about his past. Celeste said he did not have a "Gary Hart–type personal problem."[5] Days later, the *Cleveland Plain Dealer* reported that Celeste had been linked romantically to three women. Celeste, like Clinton, also decided not to run in 1988. Unlike Clinton, he never ran at all, leaving electoral politics at the end of his second term in 1991.

Democrats instead gave the nomination to Governor Michael Dukakis of Massachusetts, who led polls early but ended up losing convincingly to Vice President George H. W. Bush. Bush had a tenuous connection to Ohio: his grandfather, Samuel P. Bush, made his name in Columbus as president of the Buckeye Steel Castings Company, also serving as a president of the Ohio Manufacturers' Association and as a member of several federal commissions.[6] Samuel P. Bush's son, Prescott, was a senator from Connecticut, and Samuel's grandson and great-grandson would both serve as president.

Bush slightly overperformed his national average in Ohio, winning every county in three of the state's six regions: central, southwest, and west. A lone bright spot for Democrats was that Dukakis won the southeast, indicating that the region did not require its Democrats to be of southern origin in order to win its backing.

But being an actual southerner, one who was in some ways like Carter, couldn't hurt. Enter Clinton, who four years after declining to run emerged from another crowded Democratic field to capture the 1992 nomination.

Bush's dropping approval, despite the United States' victory against Iraq in the Persian Gulf War and the collapse of the Soviet Union, made the Democratic nomination worth having. Bush's approval rating, as measured by Gallup, was 34 percent in October 1992, similar to Carter's weak 37 percent mark the September before he lost.[7] The country was ready for a change after 12 years of Republican chief executives.

Clinton and Bush would have company on the ballot: Texas businessman Ross Perot would become the most successful third-party presidential candidate since Teddy Roosevelt in 1912, winning 19 percent of the vote and appealing largely to white voters. Perot's candidacy, *National Journal*'s John B. Judis wrote, activated what sociologist Donald Warren called the "Middle American Radicals," or MARS, voters. These voters are overwhelmingly white, generally have low-to-middle levels of income and education, and are not necessarily pro-government or pro-big business. Populists can appeal to them, and they were the kinds of voters who supported Wallace in 1968, Perot in both 1992 and 1996, commentator Pat Buchanan's insurgent Republican Party presidential primary bids in the 1990s, and real estate titan Donald Trump in his bid for the Republican nomination in 2016.[8]

In a postelection analysis, the *New York Times* noted how Perot got 23 percent of the vote in states with black populations below the national average of 12 percent, but only 13 percent in the states with above-average black populations.[9] Perot's 15 best counties by percentage in Ohio[10] were overwhelmingly white: according to the 1990 census, those counties had about 800,000 residents, of whom fewer than 10,000 were black.

Ohio was 10.7 percent black in the 1990 census, so slightly less than the nation. Sure enough, Perot overperformed in Ohio—winning 21 percent, or two points higher than his national tally—but it was only his 26th-best state. Given that 51 entities—50 states and the District of Columbia—participated in that presidential election, Ohio's Perot percentage was right at the national median in 1992.

National exit polls suggested that Perot drew roughly evenly from both Bush and Clinton in 1992, meaning that Clinton almost certainly would have won a one-on-one race. However, the outcome might have been different in at least one place: Ohio, which very well could have voted for Bush. Clinton won Ohio by only a 40.2 percent to 38.3 percent margin over Bush, or about 51 percent to 49 percent in the two-party vote, making the state about two points more Republican than the nation that year. While the exit polls indicated Perot didn't hurt or help either major-party nominee, that did not mean all Perot voters acted the same way in every state. In some states, Perot hurt Clinton. In others, Perot hurt Bush, and the exit polls indicated that was the case in Ohio.[11]

However, exit polls, just like any other poll, are imperfect. As E. J. Dionne Jr. wrote in a *Washington Post* story about the exit polls, there was nothing definitive about the analysis: "And even in Ohio, the hypothetical Bush 'margin' without Perot in the race was so small that given the normal margin of error in polls, the state still might have stuck with Clinton absent the Texas billionaire."[12]

Perot aside, Clinton slightly improved on Carter's 1976 two-party performance, winning 58 percent in both the northeast and southeast (Carter won only about 55 percent in both regions in 1976). Clinton needed this improvement in these two regions in order to improve on the Georgian's showing, because the rest of the state voted effectively the same way in both races. In the decade and a half from Carter to Clinton, the Democratic math in the state hadn't changed much: win the eastern part of the state and hold down GOP performance in the rest of it.

In 1996, Ohio played out similarly, giving Clinton a six-point win in the all-party balloting, the biggest win for a Democrat in Ohio since LBJ in 1964. Clinton defeated Republican Bob Dole and Perot, who lost about half of his support from 1992 both in Ohio and nationally. Clinton carried several counties that had not voted for a Democrat since LBJ. Most of them have small populations and would quickly revert back to Republicanism four years later, but one of them would be vital for Democrats, if not in this election, then in the battles to come. For the first time in 32 years, Franklin County (Columbus), home of the capital and its Greek Revival statehouse, voted Democratic: Clinton won it by about 3.5 points.

One of the most common observations about Franklin County one will hear—other than the suggestion that the best time to go grocery shopping is during an Ohio State football game, because the store will be largely empty—is that "nobody is from here." That's not quite true, but the city, with its vibrant private sector employers like Cardinal Health, the insurance giant Nationwide, and many others, along with the twin employment engines of OSU and the state government, has clearly been a magnet for migrants from other parts of the state and beyond for decades. As Mike Curtin, the longtime editor and associate publisher of the *Columbus Dispatch* who later won election to the state House of Representatives in 2012 as a Democrat, observed in his *Ohio Politics Almanac*, from 1960 to 2010 Columbus went from having 400,000 fewer residents than Cleveland to having 400,000 more. Part of that was due to the city's annexation of surrounding areas in exchange for water and sewer rights.

By the 2010s it was roughly six times as large as it was in 1950, making it, by land area, one of the biggest cities in the nation.[13] By 1980, Franklin County had surpassed Hamilton County as the state's second-largest source of presidential votes. It is only a matter of time before it passes Cuyahoga County in votes cast, given the trends in the early 21st century: Franklin's population grew 13.4 percent from 2000 to 2013, while Cuyahoga's contracted by 9.4 percent in the same time frame.

Like so much else about the story of Ohio's political evolution, Franklin County's transition from strongly Republican to increasingly Democratic is not a localized, unique tale. Rather, Franklin is just one of many big, urban counties across the country that have become more Democratic over time, as Republican strength has grown in exurban and rural areas while Democratic power has only grown in big cities and some suburbs.

In 1988, George H. W. Bush won 29 of the 50 most populous counties (that is, most populous in 2010, so as to compare results in the same counties across different decades). Of those 29, Bush matched or exceeded his 53.4 percent showing in the all-party voting in 22 of them. In other words, nearly half of these big, urban counties were more Republican than the nation as a whole in the late 1980s. Franklin was one of them, giving Bush an impressive 60 percent. By 2000, the Republicans would carry just 16 of these counties, and by 2012, only four.[14]

These counties generally have densely packed populations, and in this period population density was becoming a good predictor of partisan alignment. For instance, after the 2014 midterm elections, Democrats controlled 87 of the 100 smallest congressional districts by land area—in other words, the most densely populated, urban districts in places like New York City and Los Angeles—while Republicans controlled 80 of the 100 biggest congressional districts, which are less dense and rural. In the 2012 election, Barack Obama won an average of 68.3 percent of the all-party vote in the 100 small districts, while Mitt Romney won an average of 56.4 percent in the 100 biggest.

In other words, what happened to Franklin County was not unusual or distinctive. Nor would be the developments in the rest of the state that would keep it firmly anchored to the national voting in a series of four highly competitive elections in the 2000s.

The first four elections of the 21st century featured a striking amount of consistency in Ohio's county-level results. Of Ohio's 88 counties, 77 of them voted for the same party in all four elections, including 10 of the 13 counties that cast over 100,000 votes in the 2012 election (these counties account for about 60 percent of the state's total votes).[15] The next chapter will explore the individual county-level voting patterns in more detail, but of the 77 consistent counties, 12 were Democratic and 65 were Republican in all four of these elections. For decades, the Ohio Democratic vote had been concentrated—a far cry from the situation at the dawn of the 20th century, when William Jennings Bryan carried 34 counties in 1896 while losing by five points statewide—but it was now becoming more so.

For Vice President Al Gore, the Democrat who ran to succeed Clinton in 2000, his base of support in Ohio was both too concentrated and not concentrated enough. Meaning, he lost several counties that Clinton had won four years earlier, particularly in southeast Ohio, and he could not compensate for their loss with sufficient gains in the state's core Democratic areas.

Perot did not run in 2000, and the Ohio exit polls suggested that Republican nominee George W. Bush, the governor of Texas and son of the former president, benefited from his absence. Bush won about 60 percent of 1996 Perot voters, while Gore got only 30 percent. The other roughly 10 percent mostly went to Green Party nominee and consumer advocate Ralph Nader, although Pat Buchanan, the MARS-backed populist conservative commentator mentioned earlier, also got a few points' worth of Perot support in his third-party bid that year. Buchanan's best counties were largely in southeast Ohio, where in some places he won 2 percent to 3 percent of the vote despite getting just 0.6 percent statewide.

Bush would win Ohio by about 3.5 points in all-party voting over Gore despite narrowly losing the national popular vote. In the two-party vote, Ohio leaned about two points toward the Republicans, effectively in line with the state's lean in the Clinton years. Gore essentially wrote off the state late in the campaign, pulling out his resources to focus on other places, such as Florida, which Gore would lose by only 537 votes in a controversial finish. Nader's candidacy probably cost Gore Florida and, potentially, New Hampshire, either of which if flipped would have given Gore victory in the Electoral College. In Ohio, Nader's vote share was 2.5 points, so even if all those votes had gone to Gore he would have come up a point short. Nader generally won his highest percentages in Democratic-leaning counties, and college towns in particular: his 6.5 percent in Athens County, home of Ohio University, was by far his best performance in the state. Nader also did well in Portage (Kent State University) and Wood (Bowling Green State University).

The southeast Ohio two-party vote percentage was about the same as the statewide total—Bush won it and the state 52 percent to 48 percent. But remember, southeast Ohio had previously been more Democratic than the state, sometimes significantly so: the region was roughly five points or so bluer than the state overall in the elections from 1976 to 1996.

The southeast Ohio swing toward the Republicans was far from unique. Other places across Appalachia discarded their Democratic roots in 2000.

West Virginia, the only state that the Appalachian Regional Commission defines as completely Appalachian, voted Republican in 2000 for just the fourth time since the New Deal. The three previous occurrences were in the GOP landslides of 1956, 1972, and 1984. The Mountain State was so Democratic that it backed both Carter in 1980 and Dukakis in 1988 despite their big national losses. Bush's 2000 victory was no national blowout, and West Virginia would only become more Republican in subsequent elections. Gore would lose many Clinton '96 counties across the Appalachian region. The nation's poorest region—Ohio's Appalachian slice is certainly not affluent—was moving away from the nation's historic working-class party.

The reasons were many: Appalachia is very white, and the Democrats were becoming more and more the party of nonwhites, culminating in the party's 2008 nomination of the first nonwhite major party presidential nominee ever, Barack Obama. Coal mining is a significant part of much of the region's economic and cultural identity (particularly in West Virginia), and the Democrats were becoming more clearly the party of environmentalists (climate change is the issue Gore is probably most passionate about). And the Democrats were becoming more socially liberal, while Appalachia is largely rural and socially conservative. In the 2010s, roughly one in three southeast Ohioans were white evangelical Protestants, according to polling conducted by the Public Religion Research Institute. That's the highest such percentage of any of Ohio's regions.[16] White evangelical Protestants are heavily conservative and Republican across the nation, and Bush's expressions of his own evangelical faith were probably helpful to him throughout the region, just as Carter's likely were a quarter century earlier. All told, of the 10 Ohio counties where Bush made his greatest gains in the two-party vote over Dole's performance four years earlier, nine were in Appalachian Ohio.[17]

The place where Bush made his smallest two-party gain over Dole was Franklin, which would vote more Democratic than the state in 2000 for the first time since 1924. The second-smallest gain was in Hamilton, an early sign that its Republican lean was becoming less pronounced.

One could make the argument that in 2000 Ohio actually voted for the losing presidential candidate for the first time since 1960: Gore won the national vote by about half a percentage point, becoming the first presidential candidate in more than a century to lose the Electoral College while winning the overall popular vote (Democrat Grover Cleveland in 1888 was the most recent before Gore). But Bush won the presidency, and Ohio voted for him.

In 2000 the state found itself somewhat sidelined in the campaign, but Ohio would be the key state in the Electoral College four years later, when Bush narrowly dispatched Democratic nominee John Kerry, a senator from Massachusetts. Without carrying Ohio, Bush would have lost the election.

Despite a surge in two-party voting—more than one million more Ohioans cast votes for either Bush or Kerry in 2004 than had for Bush or Gore in 2000—the state's basic political geography remained largely unchanged: Bush won the state by 165,091 votes in his first election, and 118,601 in his second. One important factor that helps explain why Kerry got closer than Gore is that neither Nader, nor any other significant left-leaning third-party candidate, was on the Ohio ballot in 2004.

There are a couple of myths surrounding the 2004 election that merit comment. The first is the charge—levied by Robert F. Kennedy Jr., son of the assassinated former senator, and others—that Republicans stole the 2004 election. Kennedy's accusations have been thoroughly debunked by many others, including Farhad Manjoo of Salon.com in 2006.

Among Kennedy's dubious assertions was expressing amazement that a little-known liberal Democratic state Supreme Court candidate, C. Ellen Connally, could significantly outperform Kerry in several Republican counties. In actuality, Ohio judicial races are nonpartisan, which means voters lack the party ID cue in those contests, so it's not that surprising that some Republicans might back Bush and Connally, who they might not have known was a Democrat.

Kennedy and others pointed out that long lines at polling places might have prevented some potential voters from casting ballots, which is not a crazy point, as Manjoo concedes: "Kennedy is right to highlight the problem of long lines; every single study of the Ohio race done so far has fingered this problem as by far the single biggest cause of disenfranchisement."[18] However, it's not clear that only Democrats were disenfranchised, and the Democratic National Committee itself found that the voters who were dissuaded by long lines would have divided evenly between Bush and Kerry. J. Kenneth Blackwell, the Republican secretary of state and Democratic bogeyman at the center of some of the 2004 conspiracy theories, apparently was not actually that great at stealing elections: he lost his bid for the Ohio governorship in 2006 by 24 points. "Rigging Ohio for Bush would have required energy and skill from a secretary of state who had neither," *Plain Dealer* columnist Thomas Suddes wrote of Blackwell.[19] And secretaries of state in Ohio are not that powerful anyway: bipartisan county boards run elections in Ohio. To the extent that it was hard for some Ohioans to vote in 2004—and it was in some places— long lines and other problems were more the fault of county officials of both parties than some dark conspiracy.

Kennedy and others also cite exit polls that suggested Kerry might have won Ohio and nationally. But the pollsters who conducted the 2004 exit polls said later that they were flawed. "Procedural problems compounded by the refusal of large numbers of Republican voters to be surveyed led to inflated estimates of support for John F. Kerry," according to a *Washington Post* story on the exit pollsters' postelection self-autopsy.[20]

Another argument against a 2004 Ohio conspiracy was the preelection polling. Taken together, the surveys were very accurate. The final Real-ClearPolitics average of polls—poll averaging was coming into vogue in 2004 as a way to boil all the various state and national horse race surveys down into one easy-to-digest number—showed Bush leading by 2.1 points, exactly predicting Bush's actual 50.8 percent to 48.7 percent margin of victory over Kerry.[21]

There's little to the notion that Republicans stole Ohio in 2004. Even so, nearly a decade after the election more than a third of Democrats still believed this conspiracy theory, according to a 2013 Fairleigh Dickinson University poll.[22]

The second 2004 myth is considerably less outlandish, but probably also did not make the difference between Bush winning or losing. At the same time they were voting for president, Ohioans also voted on a statewide ballot issue (state Issue 1), a constitutional amendment outlawing same-sex marriage.

The amendment was redundant—gay marriage was already forbidden in Ohio—and even many Republicans, such as Governor Bob Taft and Senators Mike DeWine and George Voinovich, opposed the issue because it was poorly written. Still, more than three in five voters supported it, including majorities in all but one county (Athens). Some Democrats suspected that the Bush campaign had played a role in pushing several states to put same-sex marriage on the ballot in 2004. "It was entirely conceived by and brought on board by [Republican strategist] Karl Rove," Ohio Democratic operative Jerry Austin told the *Dayton Daily News* after the election, referring to the Bush campaign mastermind.[23] Rove didn't necessarily disagree with the assertion that the ballot issues in Ohio and other states helped reelect Bush. "I do think it was part and parcel of a broader fabric where this year moral values ranked higher than they traditionally do," Rove told the *New York Times* after the election.[24]

Did the same-sex marriage issue drive extra voters to the polls? Turnout increased in Ohio in 2004: 67.9 percent of eligible voters cast a ballot, up from 57.8 percent in 2000, according to voter turnout statistics maintained by Michael McDonald's United States Election Project. That roughly 10-point increase was larger than the 5.4-percentage-point increase nationally from 2000. But turnout spiked in the more competitive states overall: of the 12 decided by five points or less, including Ohio, turnout went up an average of 8.3 percent. That makes sense: both campaigns focused on many of these states, driving higher voter interest and turnout. So while Ohio's turnout increase was high even compared to the other swing states, it was not dramatically higher. There also was no correlation between a county's level of support for Issue 1 and its increase in turnout from 2000 to 2004.

Kerry gained about 550,000 votes over Gore's haul four years prior. Bush's improvement was a shade under 510,000 votes. Both sides' voters were highly motivated in 2004, and the Democrats actually added more of them. It just wasn't enough.

Paul Taylor of the Pew Research Center, writing in 2006, found some clues in the 2004 exit polling suggesting that Issue 1 might have helped Bush in Ohio by helping him make outsized gains among groups that strongly opposed gay marriage: "blacks (Bush got 16% of the black vote in Ohio in 2004, up from 9% in 2000); those who attend church more than once a week (Bush got 69% of those votes in 2004, up from 52% in 2000) and voters ages 65 and older (58% in 2004, up from 46% in 2000)."[25] There are some caveats, though.

We know, from the pollsters' own admission, that the 2004 exit polls were far from perfect, and more broadly such surveys are not perfectly precise. Bush getting 16 percent of the black vote in Ohio seems like a stretch. In two overwhelmingly black areas—East Cleveland, a Cleveland suburb, and Lincoln Heights, a small Cincinnati suburb—Bush did improve his performance from 2000, but only slightly: he won about 2 percent of the two-party vote in both places in 2000, and 4 percent in 2004. Other black areas of the state are more open to voting Republican, but such a significant shift in Ohio seems unlikely.[26]

A group of University of Florida political scientists studied the 2004 same-sex marriage ban results in Ohio and Michigan and argued that "attributing the passage of the ballot measures, the increased levels of statewide turnout, and most importantly, the reelection of Bush to the mobilization and electoral support of evangelical Protestants is overly simplistic and somewhat unfounded."[27] Another study of Ohio and other states that voted on same-sex marriage found that these ballot issues did generate extra support for Bush but that "Bush's gains from evangelicals were counterbalanced by losses among secularists, a wrinkle missed in the popular accounts of the 2004 election."[28]

It's hard to say with confidence what the precise effect of Issue 1 was, and what would have happened had it not been on the ballot. But here is where a historical perspective on Ohio is helpful. The state's voting patterns over the 30 elections from 1896 to 2012 are fairly consistent. Ohio generally votes close to the national average, and to the extent that it deviates from the national popular vote, it typically does so in a Republican direction; 2004 was one of only six times in 30 elections where the deviation came in the Democratic direction. If anything, Kerry performed a little bit better than history suggested he would, which is in and of itself an argument against the idea that Republicans rigged the state's results or that Issue 1 was the difference between Democratic defeat or victory.

Furthermore, there's nothing surprising about a Republican presidential candidate winning Ohio by about the same margin he wins nationally, which is what happened in Ohio in 2004. In fact, what would truly be surprising is if Ohio had voted for the Democratic presidential nominee in an election where the Republican presidential nominee was winning the national popular vote. That has never happened in the entire electoral history of the Republican-versus-Democratic presidential era, stretching back to 1856. Is it possible that the same-sex marriage ban helped Bush in Ohio? Sure. Would he have lost the state without it? Was it the decisive factor that led him to a 120,000-vote statewide victory? Very doubtful.

Overall, the 2004 election confirmed trends from 2000. Franklin County was only becoming more Democratic—it was six points bluer than the state after being just two points bluer four years earlier. Hamilton County voted for Bush, but it was only two points redder than the state, its smallest Republican lean since 1960. Meanwhile, the historically Democratic Ohio River counties of Belmont and Jefferson matched or surpassed their smallest Democratic leans since before the New Deal.

These trends would continue into the next election, when Bush's unpopularity and a poor economy combined to set the Democrats up for a strong election. The party's nomination was very much worth having, and Senators Barack Obama of Illinois and Hillary Clinton of New York fought a spirited primary battle, although the race at one time included several other Democrats, including quirky liberal Representative Dennis Kucinich of Ohio, who had also run unsuccessfully in 2004.

By the time of Ohio's primary—March 4—Obama was a prohibitive favorite for the nomination, and Clinton's roughly nine-point win in the Buckeye State did not change that. Obama would be the nominee, and he faced Republican Senator John McCain of Arizona in the general election.

Obama would become the first Democrat to win over 50 percent of the all-party voting in Ohio (51.4 percent) since Lyndon Johnson in 1964. While Carter (1976) and Clinton (1992 and 1996) carried the state, they did not clear 50 percent of all the votes cast in any of those years. The first nonwhite president did about 1.5 points worse in Ohio than he did nationally—53.7 percent in the two-party vote versus 52.3 percent in Ohio—and while he ran about a dozen points behind LBJ's landslide, he did copy the Texan's performance in at least one important way. Obama became the first Democratic presidential candidate since Johnson to unite the state's three most populous counties under the Democratic banner: Cuyahoga, Franklin, and Hamilton.

The story of Hamilton County's shift involves both the city of Cincinnati and the rest of the county, although the former moved more dramatically throughout the 1990s and 2000s than the latter. In 1992, Clinton won Cincinnati with 60 percent of the two-party vote. By 2004, Kerry was up to 69 percent, and then Obama won 76 percent in 2008 (and in 2012). In the rest of Hamilton County, Clinton won just 34 percent in 1992, and Kerry barely did better a dozen years later, winning just 36 percent. But Obama won 42 percent in the non-Cincinnati parts of the county. In other words, Democratic performance inside the city was significantly improving in the elections prior to 2008, but gains outside the city came largely in 2008 (and then were repeated in 2012). Obama was able to win the county by improving on Kerry's performance both inside and outside Cincinnati by about half a dozen points, bigger than his improvement on Kerry's statewide vote share from four years before. Hamilton County's trend toward the Democrats is likely similar to Franklin County's trajectory, and to the movement of most of the rest of the most populous counties across the country. Densely populated counties were generally becoming more Democratic throughout the country.

But 2008 also marked another change, this one more promising for the Republicans: For the first time since the Civil War, Hamilton County did not cast a majority of the total presidential votes in southwest Ohio, the eight-county region largely populated by residents of Cincinnati and its suburbs and exurbs.[29] The state's third-most-populous county had been losing population for decades, including a roughly 5 percent loss in the 2000s. Meanwhile, its neighboring collar counties—Butler, Clermont, and Warren—were all growing at fast clips. All three were among Ohio's 10 fastest-growing counties in the 21st century's first decade. In terms of presidential deviation, the non-Hamilton County parts of southwest Ohio hardly moved toward the Democrats at all from 2004 to 2008. Hamilton County might have been changing, but the rest of the southwest was too—and it is growing, while Hamilton is shrinking.

On the other side of the state, Obama performed worse than Kerry had in parts of southeast Ohio. It's impossible to rule out race as a part of Obama's falloff in Appalachia, but the Democratic decline in the region predates Obama, as mentioned above in the discussion of the 2000 and 2004 elections. All told, though, McCain performed about the same in the southeastern sliver as Bush had four years before, the only region in the state where Republican strength did not fall off from 2004.

Otherwise, Obama's map looked a lot like Gore's and Kerry's. The northeast continued to be the most Democratic region, while Obama also improved in the central and northwest parts of the state, capturing swingy counties around Lucas County (Toledo) like Ottawa and Wood (Bowling Green State University), as well as their neighbor, the historically more Republican-leaning Sandusky.

The 2012 election essentially reran the 2008 race, with a great level of stability both nationally and in Ohio. Obama lost just two states from his 2008 electoral map, Indiana and North Carolina, and fell just 1.7 points nationally from his 2008 national share of the two-party vote (from 53.7 percent to 52.0 percent). Still, it was odd for a reelected president to fade as oppose to grow from his first election to the second: Obama was the first since Woodrow Wilson in 1916 to win a smaller share of electoral

## 2012 Ohio Presidential Election

Romney (R). . . 2,661,407. . . . . . . 47.69%
*Obama (D) . . . 2,827,621. . . . . . . 50.67%
Other. . . . . . . . . . . 91,794. . . . . . . . 1.64%
Variance (D) . . . . 166,214. . . . . . . . 2.98%

**West Region**

| Republican | 392,716 | 56.82% |
| Democrat | 286,618 | 41.47% |
| Other | 11,803 | 1.71% |
| Variance (R) | 106,098 | 15.35% |

**Northwest Region**

| Republican | 219,742 | 45.12% |
| Democrat | 257,563 | 52.89% |
| Other | 9,709 | 1.99% |
| Variance (D) | 37,821 | 7.77% |

**Northeast Region**

| Republican | 897,007 | 41.74% |
| Democrat | 1,219,230 | 56.74% |
| Other | 32,640 | 1.52% |
| Variance (D) | 322,223 | 14.99% |

Williams, Fulton, Lucas, Ottawa, Defiance, Henry, Wood, Sandusky, Erie, Lorain, Huron, Medina, Cuyahoga, Summit, Lake, Geauga, Portage, Ashtabula, Trumbull, Mahoning, Putnam, Hancock, Seneca, Paulding, Wyandot, Ashland, Richland, Wayne, Stark, Columbiana, Van Wert, Allen, Hardin, Crawford, Holmes, Tuscarawas, Carroll, Mercer, Auglaize, Marion, Morrow, Knox, Coshocton, Harrison, Jefferson, Logan, Union, Delaware, Licking, Muskingum, Shelby, Champaign, Franklin, Guernsey, Belmont, Darke, Miami, Clark, Madison, Fairfield, Perry, Morgan, Noble, Monroe, Preble, Montgomery, Greene, Fayette, Pickaway, Hocking, Washington, Butler, Warren, Clinton, Ross, Athens, Hamilton, Clermont, Highland, Pike, Vinton, Meigs, Brown, Adams, Jackson, Scioto, Gallia, Lawrence

☐ Democratic
■ Republican

**Southwest Region**

| Republican | 481,471 | 55.80% |
| Democrat | 368,605 | 42.72% |
| Other | 12,750 | 1.48% |
| Variance (R) | 112,866 | 13.08% |

**Central Region**

| Republican | 536,181 | 47.29% |
| Democrat | 578,533 | 51.02% |
| Other | 19,220 | 1.69% |
| Variance (D) | 42,352 | 3.73% |

**Southeast Region**

| Republican | 134,290 | 52.25% |
| Democrat | 117,072 | 45.55% |
| Other | 5,672 | 2.21% |
| Variance (R) | 17,218 | 6.70% |

MAP 6.2. The 2012 presidential election in Ohio. *Source:* OhioElectionResults.com

votes in his second election than his first, and the first since Andrew Jackson in 1832 to capture a smaller percentage of the all-party popular vote. The aftereffects of the 2008 economic crisis—a crisis that helped elect Obama—dragged down his approval rating in his first term, and Obama and the Democrats expended a great deal of political capital on the Affordable Care Act, a polarizing measure designed to increase access to health insurance. The election seemed very competitive throughout the fall—Republican nominee Mitt Romney, a former Massachusetts governor, actually led in some national polls after he dominated Obama in their first debate—but the Obama campaign's internal surveys consistently suggested the president would carry Ohio and most of the key swing states, and that's precisely what happened.[30]

Southeast Ohio continued to slip away from the Democrats. Belmont and Jefferson registered their biggest Republican leans since before the New Deal, and both voted for Romney. Yet Obama's decline across Appalachia was far from universal: He actually slightly improved his performance from 2008 in several Appalachian counties, even though the only county he carried southeast of Columbus was liberal enclave Athens. For instance, Obama lost small Pike County by just a single vote, and his biggest improvement in any county (he gained three points) came in Pike's more populous northern neighbor, Ross, which is home to Chillicothe, Ohio's original capital before Columbus. Maybe some of these voters benefited from Obama's policies, or maybe they just didn't like the wealthy Romney, whom Democrats went to great lengths to paint as a plutocrat. A tongue-in-cheek lesson from 2012 could perhaps be that if a party wants to lose Ohio, it will nominate someone from Massachusetts: Romney became just the latest Bay State presidential nominee to lose Ohio, following Kennedy (1960), Dukakis (1988), and Kerry (2004).

The counties where Obama improved his share of the two-party vote from 2008 to 2012 are a rather disparate group, ranging from places like Pike and Ross south of Columbus to Franklin collar counties like Fairfield, Licking, and Pickaway to Democratic strongholds like Athens, Cuyahoga, and Franklin itself. Some of these places are diverse, urban counties, while others are rural and white. This is worth noting because there were some indications that a surge in black voting from 2008 to 2012 helped Obama hold

Ohio. For instance, the 2008 exit poll showed that Ohio's electorate was 11 percent black, while the 2012 exit poll showed a 15 percent black electorate.

That would be a noteworthy jump, but it's probably overstated to at least some extent. The national electorate was 13 percent black in both 2008 and 2012, according to the national exit poll. Ohio's black population did grow from 2008 to 2012, from 11.7 percent to 12.2 percent, but that's not enough growth to suggest such a big surge in the black electorate.

Mike Dawson didn't find much of a surge. He analyzed voting in black precincts in Akron, Cincinnati, Columbus, Dayton, and Toledo— he couldn't compare 2008 to 2012 voting in Cleveland because the city's ward and precinct boundaries were redrawn between those elections— and found that Obama's vote totals had either barely increased or slightly declined from 2008. Turnout was down across the state: Obama won about 112,000 fewer votes than he had in 2008 while Romney won about 16,400 fewer than McCain had. Dawson's results perhaps suggest that black voters turned out in relatively similar numbers in 2012 while other groups declined, which would make sense given the exit poll differences. What looked like a surge might have just been stability amidst a decline in other groups. Obama won 95 percent or more of the black vote in Ohio in both 2008 and 2012, although these voters were highly Democratic long before Obama emerged.[31]

## From Red to Blue and Blue to Red

Looking back over the 30 elections from 1896 to 2012, one can see the state's political transformation. Of the 34 counties that William Jennings Bryan, the Democrat, carried in 1896, 32 would vote for Romney in 2012. Of Ohio's 10 most vote-rich counties in 1896, Republican William McKinley carried nine. In 2012, Democrat Obama carried nine of the 10 counties that cast the most votes in that election. On both lists, the one outlier was Butler County, Hamilton's northern neighbor and part of greater Cincinnati. In 1896, Butler was 12 points more Democratic in the two-party vote than the state as a whole. In 2012, it was 14 points more Republican.

Remember Holmes County from chapter 4, the Amish enclave that had so strongly supported Clement Vallandigham in the 1863 gubernatorial race? In 1896 Holmes was Bryan's top county, followed by heavily Catholic Mercer in western Ohio. More than a century later, Romney's two best 2012 counties were Mercer and Holmes.

Despite the slow, methodical reconfiguration of Ohio's voting over the course of 30 presidential elections, Ohio's relationship to the national voting remained essentially the same in 1896 and 2012. In the former, Ohio was 0.2 points more Republican than the nation, and in 2012 it was 0.5 points redder. Ohio had changed—and the nation had changed—but Ohio's changes had by and large mirrored the nation's, keeping it tightly bound to the nation's political sentiments.

# SEVEN

*Searching for the Bellwether's Bellwether*

In the schmaltzy 1947 film *Magic Town*, pollster Lawrence "Rip" Smith, played by Jimmy Stewart, is down on his luck. His major rival has forced him out of business. But Smith holds out hope that he can find a "mathematical miracle," a place that reflects the nation so well that he'll be able to conduct accurate public opinion polling much more cheaply than by taking a national survey. He stumbles upon Grandview, a demographically perfect representation of the United States. There he poses as an insurance salesman so that his interview subjects don't know that they are being polled and thus give him candid, unspoiled answers. Smith also knows that if anything changes the character of the town, it will no longer reflect the views of the nation. To avoid that disaster, he intervenes to help prevent the city from building a civic center to attract new residents. Smith's secret gets out, however, and Grandview is flooded with pollsters and reporters, turning it from a barometer into an outlier. As political scientist Everett C. Ladd tells it, "once made self-conscious, this 'mathematically perfect community' quickly becomes representative of nothing—a doomed social science experiment."[1]

For some in the media in the late 1990s and early 2000s, Ohio's Magic Town was Canton, the state's eighth-largest city, located just down Interstate 77 from Cleveland and Akron. Home of the Pro Football Hall of Fame, Canton is the seat of Stark County, a place that often reflects statewide presidential voting.

During the 1996 campaign cycle, *New York Times* reporter Michael Winerip actually moved his family to Canton and made a "favorable impression . . . on local residents, who read his *Times* stories about their lives and thoughts in the local paper, the *Repository.*" In 2004, the *Columbia Journalism Review* noted what *Repository* editor David Kaminski called "the Winerip Effect." Kaminski had been impressed by Winerip's embedding himself in the community. He was unimpressed, however, by the copycats who arrived during the 2004 campaign, and he was "troubled by the fact that so much of the reporting emanating from his hometown by the visiting media [was] superficial."[2] Stark County voted for the Ohio and national winners in the 1996 and 2000 elections, but it misfired in 2004, backing John Kerry while the state and nation backed the winner, incumbent George W. Bush.

Clark County, part of the greater Dayton area and home to Springfield, also often reflects statewide voting patterns. In 2004, the left-leaning British newspaper the *Guardian* asked its readers to send letters to Clark County voters in order to influence the outcome. The backlash was immediate, with many county residents and other Americans telling the Brits to butt out. "We don't need weenie-spined Limeys meddling in our presidential election," wrote one.[3] If the widely covered letter-writing campaign had any effect, it was a negative one for Democrats. Clark switched to Bush in 2004, making it the only county in the state that moved from Democratic to Republican between 2000 and 2004. Perhaps, unlike in Magic Town, outside interference in Clark actually made it *more* indicative of national opinion. Still, the change was small. Al Gore won the county by about six-tenths of a point in 2000, while Bush won it by two points in 2004. Clark then voted Republican in 2008 and 2012, while the state and nation voted Democratic.

The search for a bellwether county in Ohio dates back at least to the 1930s, when pollster George Gallup identified Erie County, home of the city of Sandusky and the Cedar Point amusement park, as a great predictor not only of state-level presidential results but of national ones as well. In 1938, Gallup called Erie County, Ohio, and Summit County, Utah, "two of the best indices of national election sentiment of any of the more than 3,000 counties in the land."[4]

Erie County fascinated others, as well. In 1940, political scientists Paul Lazarsfeld, Bernard R. Berelson, and Hazel Gaudet chose Erie County for a study of voting behavior, in part because for the previous four decades it had "deviated very little from the national voting trends." They did not do so, however, because they thought Erie County necessarily reflected the views of the nation: "Because of the diversity of American life, there is no such thing as a 'typical American county,'" they wrote in *The People's Choice*, adding that they were studying the "*development* of votes and not their distribution."[5] They were not looking for Magic Town, and it's a good thing that they weren't: Erie ended up voting for the loser, Wendell Willkie, in 1940.[6] Erie voted considerably more Republican than the state throughout the middle of the 20th century, before becoming more Democratic than the state in later years.

Stark, Clark, Erie—are these bellwether Ohio counties? Or is there another magic Ohio county? Probably not.

In the 1970s, Edward Tufte and his student Richard Sand studied the idea of bellwether counties and found that counties with good records of voting for the winner or closely mirroring the national vote did not have much value in predicting the future. "Are there bellwether electoral districts? No, at least not if they are chosen before the fact," they wrote.[7] More recently, Daniel J. Coffey studied Ohio's counties and did not find a bellwether. He also suggested that small movements in some of the most closely contested counties don't really change outcomes in elections, both because they are dwarfed by changes in bigger counties and because, since there is no statewide Electoral College, "there isn't a prize for racking up county victories."[8]

A detailed look at the presidential performance of each of Ohio's 88 counties indicates a lack of an obvious bellwether. Table 7.1 lists all the Ohio counties in order of their average presidential deviation from state results over the last 30 elections—essentially, a county-level version of the state-level statistics cited in chapter 2. The lower the deviation, the closer the county was to the statewide average. This table also includes the number of times over the last 30 elections that the county voted with the statewide winner.

## Table 7.1. Average two-party presidential deviation by county and number of times each county has voted with the state and national winners, 1896–2012

| County | Avg. two-party state deviation | Avg. national deviation | No. of times voted with state winner | No. of times voted with national winner | County | Avg. two-party state deviation | Avg. national deviation | No. of times voted with state winner | No. of times voted with national winner |
|---|---|---|---|---|---|---|---|---|---|
| Montgomery | 2.4 | 3 | 24 | 24 | Seneca | 8 | 8.6 | 20 | 18 |
| Stark | 2.4 | 3.1 | 24 | 24 | Champaign | 8.1 | 9.5 | 21 | 19 |
| Clark | 2.8 | 4 | 21 | 21 | Knox | 8.1 | 9.6 | 21 | 19 |
| Perry | 3 | 4.2 | 23 | 21 | Medina | 8.1 | 9.6 | 21 | 19 |
| Portage | 3.3 | 4.1 | 26 | 26 | Fayette | 8.2 | 9.4 | 22 | 20 |
| Tuscarawas | 3.5 | 4.1 | 23 | 23 | Meigs | 8.2 | 9.7 | 22 | 20 |
| Erie | 3.6 | 3.8 | 25 | 23 | Athens | 8.5 | 9.6 | 21 | 19 |
| Hocking | 3.6 | 4 | 26 | 24 | Pickaway | 8.5 | 8.9 | 19 | 17 |
| Franklin | 3.9 | 5.5 | 24 | 22 | Belmont | 8.7 | 7.8 | 20 | 22 |
| Scioto | 4 | 5 | 24 | 22 | Clermont | 8.7 | 10.1 | 20 | 18 |
| Ross | 4.3 | 5.4 | 25 | 23 | Morgan | 8.9 | 9.8 | 20 | 18 |
| Vinton | 4.8 | 5.6 | 23 | 21 | Butler | 9 | 9.2 | 19 | 19 |
| Columbiana | 4.9 | 6 | 24 | 22 | Defiance | 9 | 9.6 | 19 | 17 |
| Guernsey | 5.1 | 6.8 | 24 | 22 | Wayne | 9 | 9.8 | 20 | 18 |
| Hamilton | 5.1 | 6.3 | 24 | 22 | Darke | 9.2 | 10.2 | 20 | 18 |
| Ottawa | 5.2 | 5.3 | 25 | 23 | Madison | 9.3 | 10.6 | 21 | 19 |
| Muskingum | 5.3 | 6.8 | 21 | 19 | Morrow | 9.3 | 10.7 | 21 | 19 |
| Lorain | 5.4 | 5.8 | 21 | 23 | Jefferson | 9.6 | 9.5 | 18 | 20 |
| Wood | 5.4 | 6.8 | 24 | 22 | Fairfield | 9.7 | 10.6 | 19 | 17 |
| Marion | 5.6 | 6.9 | 20 | 18 | Trumbull | 9.8 | 9.4 | 17 | 19 |
| Jackson | 5.8 | 7.5 | 22 | 20 | Gallia | 9.9 | 11.1 | 20 | 18 |
| Lawrence | 5.8 | 6.8 | 25 | 23 | Van Wert | 10 | 10.5 | 21 | 19 |
| Lake | 5.9 | 7.2 | 22 | 22 | Cuyahoga | 10.2 | 9.3 | 22 | 24 |
| Coshocton | 6 | 7 | 21 | 19 | Allen | 10.4 | 11.6 | 19 | 17 |
| Adams | 6.1 | 7.2 | 23 | 21 | Mahoning | 10.4 | 10.3 | 20 | 22 |
| Harrison | 6.2 | 7.3 | 21 | 19 | Williams | 10.5 | 11.2 | 21 | 19 |
| Summit | 6.4 | 6.3 | 21 | 23 | Monroe | 10.6 | 10 | 16 | 14 |
| Richland | 6.5 | 7.3 | 21 | 19 | Wyandot | 10.7 | 11.4 | 19 | 17 |
| Huron | 6.7 | 7.8 | 24 | 22 | Shelby | 10.8 | 10.9 | 18 | 16 |
| Noble | 6.8 | 8.2 | 22 | 20 | Delaware | 10.9 | 12.3 | 20 | 18 |
| Pike | 6.8 | 5.8 | 19 | 21 | Ashland | 11.4 | 12.5 | 19 | 17 |
| Sandusky | 6.8 | 7.6 | 23 | 21 | Logan | 11.4 | 12.8 | 20 | 18 |
| Licking | 6.9 | 8.4 | 21 | 19 | Geauga | 11.5 | 13.3 | 20 | 18 |
| Lucas | 7 | 6.8 | 24 | 24 | Crawford | 11.6 | 12.2 | 18 | 16 |
| Paulding | 7 | 7.5 | 21 | 19 | Clinton | 11.7 | 13.2 | 19 | 17 |
| Washington | 7 | 8.4 | 21 | 19 | Warren | 11.7 | 13.4 | 19 | 17 |
| Carroll | 7.3 | 8.9 | 22 | 20 | Hancock | 12.3 | 13.4 | 21 | 19 |
| Greene | 7.4 | 9 | 20 | 18 | Union | 12.9 | 14.3 | 20 | 18 |
| Preble | 7.4 | 8.7 | 23 | 21 | Fulton | 13.1 | 14.4 | 19 | 17 |
| Hardin | 7.5 | 8.4 | 23 | 21 | Auglaize | 13.3 | 13.6 | 19 | 17 |
| Ashtabula | 7.6 | 8.6 | 22 | 20 | Henry | 13.3 | 13.4 | 19 | 17 |
| Highland | 7.6 | 8.8 | 23 | 21 | Mercer | 13.6 | 13.5 | 17 | 15 |
| Miami | 7.8 | 9.3 | 21 | 19 | Holmes | 15.7 | 16.5 | 18 | 16 |
| Brown | 7.9 | 8.1 | 20 | 18 | Putnam | 15.9 | 16.1 | 18 | 16 |

None of these counties has a presidential deviation more closely matching the national vote than does the state as a whole. Ohio's average deviation was 2.2 points, and the smallest deviation of any county was three points (Montgomery County). Additionally, no county matches the state's overall record of voting with the national winner in 28 of the last 30 elections.

These data suggest that searching for an Ohio version of Magic Town is probably a waste of time. In fact, over the last four elections, the most competitive Ohio counties have not decided the outcome. The state's vast swath of rural and suburban Republican strength powered George W. Bush to victories in 2000 and 2004, while its areas of mostly urban Democratic might struck back in 2008 and 2012 by voting for Barack Obama. Defining those respective areas of partisan strength, as well as the swing counties, is the goal of the rest of this chapter.

As noted previously, 2000 through 2012 was a time of great stability in Ohio voting, with two-party voting lying within a narrow band. In elections during this period, the Republicans won a high of just 51.8 percent of the two-party vote (2000) and a low of 47.7 percent (2008), while the Democrats shifted between a high of 52.3 percent (2008) and a low of 48.2 percent (2000).

The state's 88 counties can be divided into three politically like-minded units. These are the Purple Enclaves (the most competitive counties), the Blue Islands (the most Democratic counties), and the Red Reach (the most Republican counties). There are 20 counties in the purple group, 10 in the blue group, and a whopping 58 (about two-thirds of the total) in the red group. This apparent sea of red is certainly not unique to Ohio. Even in his reelection victory in 2012, Barack Obama won only 22 percent of the nation's counties, and just 28 percent four years earlier.[9] In 2012, Obama won 17 Ohio counties (19 percent of the state's total) and 22 (25 percent) in 2008. Here again, Ohio's voting pattern reflected that of the nation.

Map 7.1 shows Ohio's counties shaded by their status as part of the Blue Islands, Purple Enclaves, or Red Reach. The Blue Islands are counties in which the Democratic presidential nominees from 2000 to 2012—Al Gore, John Kerry, and Barack Obama (twice)—won 55 percent or more

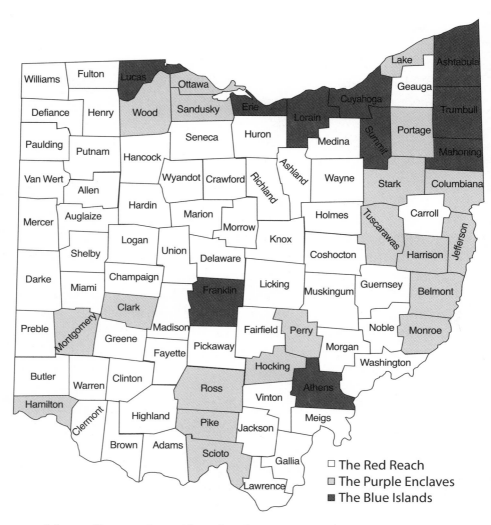

MAP 7.1. Democratic presidential performance by Ohio county, 2000–2012

of the combined and rounded two-party vote. The Purple Enclaves are counties in which the Democratic nominees won between 46 and 54 percent, and the Red Reach represents the counties in which the Democratic nominees captured 45 percent or less, which means the Republican nominees—George W. Bush (twice), John McCain, and Mitt Romney—won a combined 55 percent or more.

## Table 7.2. Combined 2000–2012 presidential voting by county blocs

|  | '00–'12 Republican votes | '00–'12 Democratic votes | Total votes | Democratic % | % of votes cast '00–'12 |
|---|---|---|---|---|---|
| Blue Islands | 3,160,583 | 5,106,074 | 8,266,657 | 61.8% | 38.9% |
| Purple Enclaves | 2,925,835 | 2,934,054 | 5,859,889 | 50.1% | 27.6% |
| Red Reach | 4,463,816 | 2,654,982 | 7,118,798 | 37.3% | 33.5% |
| TOTAL '00–'12 | 10,550,234 | 10,695,110 | 21,245,344 | 50.3% | 100% |

The four elections, taken together, show how closely contested the state has been and provide more evidence for its special status as a mirror of the national average, albeit with a slightly red (Republican) tint. Over the course of these contests, Democratic candidates won 51.3 percent of all two-party votes cast nationally, compared to 48.7 percent for the Republicans. This average reflects the bigger victories won by Barack Obama in 2008 and 2012 as well as the closer contests won by George W. Bush in 2000 and 2004. Over the same period, the Democratic candidates won 50.3 percent of the vote in Ohio, making Ohio a point more Republican than the nation.

The diametrically opposed Red and Blue competitors effectively hold each other to a stalemate, and an almost perfectly neutral Purple group balances in the middle. As shown in table 7.2, the blue bloc casts a larger percentage of the state's total votes than does the red bloc, but it is not quite as Democratic as the red bloc is Republican. The Red Reach's Republican share of the two-party vote is 62.7 percent, a point redder than the Blue Islands' Democratic vote. The Purple Enclaves, meanwhile, cast fewer votes than either of the more partisan blocs—but these counties, combined, have split almost exactly down the middle in the last four elections. The Democrats won the combined vote in the Purple Enclaves—about 5.9 million votes cast over four elections—by fewer than 10,000 votes total.

To describe county-level voting, it is useful to compare each county's results to those of the particular state whose profile it most closely matches. For instance, Cuyahoga County, the largest source of two-party votes from 2000 to 2012, gave 68.1 percent of its votes to Democrats. The state whose voting pattern it most closely mirrored was Hawaii, which cast 65.1 percent of its two-party votes for Democrats during this period.

The 20 most competitive counties in Ohio form the Purple Enclaves. In the four elections held from 2000 to 2012, Democrat presidential candidates won the Purple Enclaves by an average of just 50.1 percent to 49.9 percent. If this group of counties were a state, its voting would have most resembled Florida's (49.9 percent Democratic) and, yes, Ohio's (50.3 percent).

Montgomery County (Dayton) is usually at least slightly more Democratic than the state overall, to the point that, if any Democrat loses it, that candidate has lost all hope of capturing an advantage in two-party votes in the state overall. Since the New Deal, Montgomery has voted Republican in just six of 21 presidential elections, all years when Democrats lost the state: 1952, 1956, 1960, 1972, 1984, and 1988.

### Table 7.3. The Purple Enclaves

| County | Democratic % 2000–2012 | % of total vote 2012 | Votes most like |
|--------|------------------------|----------------------|-----------------|
| Portage | 53.4% | 1.4% | New Mexico |
| Monroe | 52.5% | 0.1% | Wisconsin |
| Montgomery | 51.9% | 4.9% | Iowa |
| Belmont | 51.5% | 0.6% | Iowa |
| Jefferson | 51.0% | 0.6% | Colorado |
| Stark | 50.8% | 3.3% | Colorado |
| Ottawa | 50.6% | 0.4% | Colorado |
| Wood | 49.7% | 1.1% | Virginia |
| Hamilton | 49.7% | 7.6% | Virginia |
| Clark | 49.4% | 1.2% | Virginia |
| Lake | 49.1% | 2.1% | Virginia |
| Pike | 48.8% | 0.2% | Virginia |
| Sandusky | 48.3% | 0.5% | Missouri |
| Perry | 48.1% | 0.3% | Missouri |
| Scioto | 48.0% | 0.6% | Missouri |
| Hocking | 47.7% | 0.2% | Missouri |
| Harrison | 46.9% | 0.1% | North Carolina |
| Columbiana | 46.6% | 0.9% | North Carolina |
| Ross | 46.6% | 0.6% | North Carolina |
| Tuscarawas | 46.4% | 0.8% | North Carolina |
| TOTAL | 50.1% | 27.6% | Florida |

Montgomery County is the true Democratic canary in the coal mine—if it dies, the Democrats die, electorally speaking. Its neighbor to the northeast, Clark County (Springfield), typically votes close to the statewide average, though it leans more often to the right, a fact that over-zealous British letter-writers discovered first-hand in 2004.

Stark County (Canton), noted above as a favorite (if fallacious) national bellwether, voted generally more Republican for much of the second half of the 20th century before settling in close to the state average in the 21st. A big swing one way or the other in Stark probably indicates that the beneficiary of that swing is winning the state.

A few decades ago, the notion of Hamilton (Cincinnati) being a swing county would have seemed laughable. Throughout most of the second half of the 20th century, it was among the more Republican counties in the state, consistently by five or more points above the state average. It has slowly become more competitive, to the extent that, like so many other large urban counties across the country, it appears to be moving toward the Democrats. It's fitting that over the first four elections of the 21st century, Hamilton County's voting has mirrored most closely that of Virginia, a state that is moving in much the same way. Virginia, like Hamilton County, had not voted Democratic in any presidential election from 1968 to 2004, before going for Obama twice. Both Virginia the state and Hamilton the county may well remain closely aligned to the national vote, but for now they seem to be trending toward the Democratic camp.

Many other Purple Enclaves are moving in a clear direction. Several Appalachian counties—Belmont, Columbiana (Salem), Harrison, Hocking, Jefferson (Steubenville), Monroe, Perry, Pike, Ross (Chillicothe), Scioto (Portsmouth), and Tuscarawas (Dover/New Philadelphia)—have either experienced at least small Republican leans, for some time, or moved that way between 2000 and 2012. This is not a surprising result, given the Democrats' overall troubles in Appalachia in the post-Clinton era.

Lake County (Mentor/Willoughby) typically leans slightly Republican, while Portage County (Kent State University) leans slightly Democratic. Both are part of the so-called Cuyahoga County collar. These six counties in all—purple Lake and Portage, blue Summit and Lorain, red Geauga and Medina—would constitute, if combined, the most populous county in Ohio, casting about 13 percent of the state's ballots (Cuyahoga's collar counties therefore collectively outvoting Cuyahoga itself). It would be a Purple Enclave, albeit one with a Democratic lean (52.8 percent Democratic, 2000–2012). Cuyahoga has long been Ohio's most populous and most Democratic county, and the Democratic lean of its collar counties is well established. Together, they anchor Democratic strength in the northeast.

The three other Purple Enclave counties are part of Greater Toledo: Ottawa (Port Clinton), Sandusky (Fremont)[10], and Wood (Bowling Green State University). The latter two had often leaned a little (or a lot) toward the Republicans, before coming to reflect the statewide vote in 2008 and 2012.

Ottawa, by the way, holds a unique position among Ohio counties. Ohio voted for the winner in every presidential election from 1964 to 2012, and Ottawa is the only Ohio county that can say the same.

## GROUP TWO: THE BLUE ISLANDS

The Blue Islands are the 10 Ohio counties in which Democratic presidential candidates received at least 55 percent of the two-party vote from 2000 to 2012. In order to win the state, Democrats must not only win all 10 of these counties, but must run up the score in every one.

### Table 7.4. The Blue Islands

| County | Democratic % 2000–2012 | % of total vote 2000–2012 | Votes most like |
|--------|------------------------|---------------------------|-----------------|
| Cuyahoga | 68.1% | 11.9% | Hawaii |
| Athens | 64.7% | 0.5% | Hawaii |
| Mahoning | 63.5% | 2.3% | Vermont |
| Lucas | 63.1% | 3.9% | Massachusetts |
| Trumbull | 61.9% | 1.9% | New York |
| Franklin | 57.3% | 9.6% | New Jersey |
| Lorain | 57.3% | 2.5% | New Jersey |
| Summit | 57.3% | 4.8% | New Jersey |
| Ashtabula | 54.9% | 0.8% | Michigan |
| Erie | 54.9% | 0.7% | Michigan |
| TOTAL | 61.8% | 38.9% | New York |

Cuyahoga County (Cleveland), of course, leads this group. It is both the state's most consistently Democratic county and the one that, as of 2012, casts the most votes in the state. It's easy to forget, though, that Cuyahoga's sheer size makes it a rich source of Republican votes as well: In 2012, it produced the third-most votes for Mitt Romney of any Ohio county. Franklin County (Columbus), the state's second-richest source of votes, gave Romney his largest vote total of any county. The only election in the two-party era (beginning in 1856) in which Franklin gave more than 60 percent of its votes to a Democrat was 2012, another sign of an ongoing Democratic trend.

Cuyahoga and Franklin are two counties headed in opposite directions. Throughout the first decade and a half of the 21st century, Cuyahoga's population contracted by close to 10 percent, while Franklin's grew by more than 10 percent. Politically opposed for much of the 20th century, they are now becoming more like allies.

Unfortunately for Democrats, many of the other counties in the Blue Islands are also losing population: Summit (Akron) experienced a slight decline in the first part of the century, while Mahoning (Youngstown) and its northern neighbor Trumbull (Warren) were losing population at nearly the rate of Cuyahoga. Ashtabula and Erie (Sandusky) Counties are also shrinking to some degree, and they barely make inclusion on this list: they get to 55 percent Democratic only by rounding up. Still, as of 2012 they had voted Democratic for seven and six straight elections, respectively.

Athens County (Ohio University), as mentioned at the end of chapter 4, has been reliably Democratic since 18-year-olds won the right to vote in advance of the 1972 election. Lucas County (Toledo), another recent population loser, was in many elections during the latter half of the 20th century and into the 21st the only Democratic county in the northwestern part of the state.

Lorain County (Elyria/Lorain), Cuyahoga's western neighbor, is growing and taking in some of those who have been leaving places closer to Cleveland. It has been reliably a half-dozen points or so more Democratic than the state for most of the postwar era.

In presidential election years, reporters and analysts commonly cite a certain margin of victory needed in Cuyahoga County in order to win

Ohio. As the *Cincinnati Enquirer* noted in the aftermath of the 1992 election, "Traditional political theory in Ohio requires a Democrat to win Cuyahoga County by 100,000 votes to buffer 'downstate' GOP strength and secure a statewide victory."[11] The dictum was true that year—Bill Clinton won Cuyahoga by about 150,000 votes—but it has also frequently been proved false. Jimmy Carter narrowly won Ohio while falling in Cuyahoga about 6,500 votes short of the mythic 100,000-vote margin. Democrats Franklin Roosevelt (1944), John F. Kennedy (1960), and Michael Dukakis (1988) all won Cuyahoga by six figures but lost the state. In 2000, Al Gore carried Cuyahoga by about 168,000 votes but didn't win Ohio. In 2004, John Kerry won Cuyahoga by about 227,000 votes and still lost. But Barack Obama cleared 255,000-vote pluralities in the county in both 2008 and 2012. So is 250,000 the new rule?

The better way to look at Ohio Democratic voting is to focus not only on Cuyahoga but also on the nine other counties that make up the Blue Islands. In 2000 and 2004, the Democratic pluralities in these counties were 300,576 and 450,928, respectively, not enough for a Democratic victory. Obama won the counties by nearly 600,000 votes in both 2008 and 2012. The true threshold for Democrats in these 10 counties is impossible to pinpoint precisely, but it's probably north of 500,000.

If the Blue Islands were a state, only five other states—Hawaii, Rhode Island, Vermont, Massachusetts, and New York—and the District of Columbia would have been more Democratic over the four elections analyzed here.

## Group Three: The Red Reach

The 58 counties that make up the Red Reach have relatively small populations. Only one, Butler County (Hamilton, Miami University), ranks in the state's top 10 for population. But together they cast about a third of the state's votes in presidential elections, acting as a counterweight to the Blue Islands.

GOP presidential nominees won at least 55 percent of the total votes cast in these counties from 2000 to 2012. None voted Democratic in any of those elections, and most have been very Republican for a very long

## Table 7.5.  The Red Reach

| County | Democratic % 2000–2012 | % of total vote 2012 | Votes most like | County | Democratic % 2000–2012 | % of total vote 2012 | Votes most like |
|---|---|---|---|---|---|---|---|
| Guernsey | 44.8% | 0.3% | Georgia | Gallia | 37.9% | 0.2% | Alaska |
| Vinton | 44.7% | 0.1% | Georgia | Crawford | 37.9% | 0.4% | Alaska |
| Muskingum | 44.6% | 0.7% | Indiana | Wyandot | 37.8% | 0.2% | Alaska |
| Carroll | 44.6% | 0.2% | Indiana | Madison | 37.8% | 0.3% | Alaska |
| Seneca | 44.1% | 0.5% | Indiana | Knox | 37.4% | 0.5% | Nebraska |
| Morgan | 44.1% | 0.1% | Indiana | Brown | 37.2% | 0.4% | Nebraska |
| Huron | 44.1% | 0.4% | Indiana | Morrow | 36.9% | 0.3% | Nebraska |
| Marion | 44.1% | 0.5% | Indiana | Delaware | 36.6% | 1.5% | Nebraska |
| Coshocton | 44.0% | 0.3% | South Carolina | Adams | 36.5% | 0.2% | Nebraska |
| Lawrence | 43.9% | 0.5% | South Carolina | Butler | 36.2% | 3.0% | Oklahoma |
| Medina | 43.6% | 1.5% | South Carolina | Allen | 36.0% | 0.9% | Oklahoma |
| Defiance | 41.4% | 0.3% | South Dakota | Ashland | 35.2% | 0.4% | Oklahoma |
| Fulton | 41.2% | 0.4% | South Dakota | Highland | 35.1% | 0.3% | Oklahoma |
| Washington | 41.1% | 0.5% | South Dakota | Miami | 34.7% | 0.9% | Oklahoma |
| Richland | 41.0% | 1.1% | Texas | Preble | 34.1% | 0.4% | Oklahoma |
| Licking | 40.5% | 1.4% | Kentucky | Logan | 34.0% | 0.4% | Oklahoma |
| Meigs | 40.4% | 0.2% | Kentucky | Hancock | 33.4% | 0.6% | Idaho |
| Jackson | 40.3% | 0.2% | Kentucky | Union | 33.0% | 0.4% | Idaho |
| Noble | 40.1% | 0.1% | Kentucky | Clinton | 32.3% | 0.3% | Idaho |
| Paulding | 40.0% | 0.2% | Kansas | Clermont | 31.5% | 1.6% | Wyoming |
| Geauga | 39.7% | 0.9% | Kansas | Van Wert | 31.5% | 0.3% | Wyoming |
| Greene | 39.6% | 1.4% | Kansas | Darke | 30.7% | 0.5% | Wyoming |
| Williams | 39.5% | 0.3% | Kansas | Shelby | 30.3% | 0.4% | Wyoming |
| Fairfield | 39.3% | 1.2% | North Dakota | Warren | 29.6% | 1.8% | Wyoming |
| Wayne | 39.3% | 0.9% | North Dakota | Auglaize | 27.2% | 0.4% | Utah |
| Pickaway | 39.0% | 0.4% | Alabama | Mercer | 25.9% | 0.4% | Utah |
| Champaign | 38.8% | 0.3% | Alabama | Putnam | 25.1% | 0.3% | Utah |
| Hardin | 38.3% | 0.2% | Alaska | Holmes | 24.9% | 0.2% | Utah |
| Henry | 38.1% | 0.3% | Alaska | | | | |
| Fayette | 37.9% | 0.2% | Alaska | TOTAL | 37.3% | 33.5% | Nebraska |

time. Of the 58, 44 have consistently voted Republican since Lyndon Johnson's 83-county landslide in 1964. Fully half of Ohio counties did not vote Democratic a single time from 1968 to 2012.[12]

Delaware County, which lies just north of Franklin and contains a small portion of Columbus thanks to the capital's slowly expanding borders,[13] is arguably Ohio's most reliably Republican county; it has voted Republican in every presidential election since 1916, the longest such streak in the state. It's also the fastest-growing county in the state, more than tripling in population from about 54,000 in 1980 to more than 180,000 in the mid-2010s. The county remains quite Republican (its lean toward the GOP has been in the double digits in every election since 1936), but it moved a couple of points toward the Democrats, relative to the state, in Obama's two elections. That movement may be only a blip, or it may indicate something more significant as time moves on. If anything, it suggests that Delaware's massive population growth is far from exclusively Republican.

Butler, Clermont (Loveland), and Warren (Mason/Lebanon) are the collar counties that circle Hamilton. The three can be considered almost as a single entity, a Republican super-county. This mutant county—let's call it "Warlermont"—would have cast 6.4 percent of the state's total votes from 2000 to 2012, a greater share than any actual county other than Cuyahoga, Franklin, or Hamilton. And Warlermont would have given about 67 percent of those votes to Republicans. Interpreting Cincinnati's exurbs in this way indicates how Ohio's Republican counties function overall: not as a series of little pieces, but as one hefty force, powerful enough to overwhelm the Democratic strongholds across the state.

Franklin's six collar counties—Delaware, Fairfield (Lancaster), Licking (Newark), Madison (London), Pickaway (Circleville), and Union (Marysville)—are all Republican, although not quite as rightward-leaning as their fellow members of the Red Reach in the southwest. Republicans won 62 percent of the votes cast in these counties. While all of these counties are growing, they don't vote with quite the same weight as Warlermont: they cast 5.3 percent of the state's votes in the last four elections.

Cuyahoga's collars contain reliably Republican counties Geauga (Chardon) and Medina (Brunswick). The other collar counties, however, contain many more votes in the aggregate than either Franklin or Hamilton, and they lean much more Democratic, as noted in the Purple Enclaves section above.

One reason why Hamilton's collar counties are more Republican than those that circle Cuyahoga or Franklin is religious. According to the Public Religion Research Institute's American Values Atlas, about a

quarter of those who live in the Cincinnati metro area are white evangelical Christians. That's a more significant percentage than in the Columbus
(18 percent) and Cleveland (15 percent) metro areas.[14] In 2012, about 30
percent of Ohio voters were white evangelicals according to exit polls,
and they backed Romney over Obama by about a 70–30 margin. Meanwhile, the roughly 70 percent of Ohioans who were not white evangelicals
backed Obama by about a 60–40 spread.[15]

Election analysis in Ohio, as suggested in the previous section, sometimes focuses overmuch on what Democrats need to do in the urban
counties, particularly Cuyahoga. So what must Republicans do in the
Red Reach to win statewide? In their 2000 and 2004 victories, Republicans won the Reach by margins of 411,535 and an eye-popping 536,473,
respectively. In their 2008 and 2012 losses, their margins were 400,865 and
459,961, respectively.

What does that make for a goal for Republicans in their best counties?
It's probably right around 500,000 votes, the same magic margin that the
Democrats need in their secure counties. If the Red Reach were a state,
it would have been more Republican from 2000 to 2012 than every other
state but four: Utah, Wyoming, Idaho, and Oklahoma. One other thing
about the Red Reach: the 10 counties with the state's highest median incomes are all part of this group.[16]

### RED VERSUS BLUE, WITH A PURPLE BYSTANDER

This is all a long way of saying that there really isn't a bellwether county
in Ohio. Places like Canton and Dayton are great for finding a politically
diverse cross-section of Ohioans, but one should not expect the statewide
winner to automatically carry Montgomery, Stark, or several other counties, like Ottawa, that are typically closely contested.

Bush won the Purple Enclaves in 2000 and 2004, and Obama won
them in 2008 and 2012. So did the purple counties decide those elections?
No. The purple counties, as a whole, are so competitive that they largely
canceled each other out in all four elections, to the point that if none of
them had cast a single vote from 2000 to 2012 the statewide winner would
not have changed in any of those elections.

In 2000 and 2004, Bush won in the Red Reach by a greater margin than he lost by in the Blue Islands, and in 2008 and 2012 Obama won the Blue Islands by a greater margin than he lost by in the Red Reach. The Purple Enclaves ended up backing the winner, but the voting in the other, more partisan parts of the state was enough to determine the victors.

That's not to say that the Purple Enclaves are unimportant. Rather, it's just to note that in the early 21st century, running up the margins in the red or the blue counties was more important for both parties to claim victory. After all, a vote in a 50–50 county counts just as much as one in a 75–25 county. Winning or losing a county by a vote doesn't mean anything. Winning or losing the state by one vote could mean everything. The parties just need to figure out where to get those votes, which—unlike electoral votes—they can get from the bluest and the reddest places alike.

# CONCLUSION

## *Will Ohio Remain a Bellwether*
## *(and Will It Lose Anything If It Doesn't)?*

Theodore Roosevelt offered one of the most famous and humorous descriptions of Ohio's electoral peculiarities: "I think there is only one thing in the world I can't understand, and that is Ohio politics."[1] The state's internal politics may be vexing at times—particularly to Democrats, who by 2018 will have held the governorship for only four of the previous 28 years—but its presidential politics over the course of the 20th century and into the early years of the 21st actually are fairly easy to understand.

In nearly every presidential election, Ohio is a bellwether in the sense that it reflects the national vote, whether that election is competitive or uncompetitive overall. In the majority of contests, Ohio is at least a little more Republican than the nation, but not *so* Republican that Democrats believe they cannot win the state. The old phrase "As Ohio goes, so goes the nation" would be just as accurate—perhaps even more accurate—if flipped around, as elections analyst Nate Silver did in 2011: "As the nation goes, so goes Ohio."[2]

From its very beginnings in 1803, Ohio was the first true melting pot for a nation that came to be defined by the concept. Societal changes in the nation as a whole, such as urbanization, immigration from Europe, and the growth of the black population outside the South, happened in Ohio, too. In the 1980s and 1990s, Ohio's tourism slogan was "Ohio: The

Heart of It All." As Al Tuchfarber, the founder of the University of Cincinnati's Ohio Poll, put it in a late 1980s assessment of the state, "The Heart of It All" was "an appropriate description for the state in the arena of presidential politics."[3] The state later junked the slogan, but it still aptly describes its place in the battle for the presidency.

Although the Republican Party has never won the White House without Ohio, the Democrats have done so five times in the two-party era (1856, 1884, 1892, 1944, and 1960). Ohio's position in the presidential derby can best be described as a necessary but not sufficient condition for Republican victory and as a sufficient but unnecessary condition for Democratic victory. This has been true ever since the founding of the GOP before the Civil War, and it seems reasonable to expect that it will remain true as the 21st century unfolds.

## THE ELECTORAL COLLEGE'S FUTURE SHAPE

In presidential elections, Ohio is the gateway to the Midwest, a region that is losing electoral votes to the Sun Belt but that is still vital to assembling an Electoral College majority. Other than Indiana, Ohio historically has been more Republican than its other midwestern neighbors, such as Illinois, Iowa, Michigan, Minnesota, and Wisconsin. All have been consistently more Democratic than Ohio, particularly Illinois, which as of the mid-2010s Republicans did not consider a plausible Electoral College target. One of these states someday may become more Republican than Ohio, but there's little evidence in past trends to predict such an outcome. Republicans would like to add Pennsylvania, Ohio's neighbor to the east, to their Electoral College coalition, but it went Democratic from 1992 to 2012 and has not voted more Republican than Ohio since 1948. Again, there may come a time when Pennsylvania votes more Republican than Ohio, but there was no sign of any such change in the early 21st century.

Going into the 2016 election, Republicans face a growing demographic challenge. Already hopelessly lost among black voters, who have given 90-plus percent of their votes to Democratic presidential candidates for decades, the party also faces deficits with two other minority groups, Hispanics and Asian Americans, whose voting strength is increasing with each year. The former, a major factor in fast-growing swing states like Colorado, Florida, and Nevada, and 10 percent of the overall electorate in 2012, gave Republican nominee Mitt Romney barely a quarter of their votes, according to the national exit poll. The latter group, although only 3 percent of the national electorate, gave Barack Obama more than 70 percent of its votes. Each group has been trending Democratic, and Obama improved his standing with both from 2008 to 2012 despite declining nationally overall, according to the exit polls (to be taken with a grain of salt).

According to census data, Ohio's African-American population was proportionately slightly smaller than that of the nation as a whole in the mid-2010s, 12.6 percent versus 13.2 percent. But the state, overall, was much whiter than the nation, about 80 percent non-Hispanic white versus 62 percent nationally. Ohio's population was just 3.5 percent Hispanic or Latino, as opposed to 17.4 percent nationally. Additionally, Ohio was just 2 percent Asian American, while the nation was 5.4 percent. Both of these minority groups were growing in Ohio throughout the first half of the 2010s, but not as quickly as they were nationally. If Ohio were to lose its bellwether status in presidential politics in the third decade of the 21st century and beyond, it might be because the state's population has only small percentages of Hispanics and Asian Americans.

One could imagine a future in which both parties' geographic areas of strength have shifted from where they are today. Democrats already have made impressive gains in historically Republican and conservative Virginia, where the growth of minority groups and the expansion of Democratic-leaning urban areas (particularly around Washington, DC) have turned that state into battleground territory. Virginia eventually may become as reliably Democratic as states like New Jersey and New York, as it effectively transitions from a conservative southern state to a moderate-to-liberal mid-Atlantic state. As of 2012, only about half of Virginia's residents had been born in the state, and many of the transplants were from parts of the country historically more liberal than the Old Dominion. By contrast, three-quarters of Ohio's population had been born in the state.[4] North Carolina and Georgia remained more Republican than the nation as a whole in both the 2008 and 2012 elections, but eventually they may move the way of Virginia as well because they are changing in similar ways. The Hispanic vote in New Mexico already had moved that state away from the Republicans, and Florida and Nevada may be next.

The Republicans could compensate for the potential loss of these states by improving their numbers in the Midwest, including not only Ohio but also Iowa, Michigan, Minnesota, and Wisconsin, which are generally whiter than the nation as a whole. Perhaps American politics may become even more racially polarized, as the growth of nonwhite voters (many expected nonwhites to cast about three of every 10 votes in 2016, eclipsing 2012's all-time high for minority participation) is balanced out by an ever-increasing shift of the white vote toward the Republicans. In 2012, Romney won about 60 percent of the white vote nationally, and perhaps Republicans can draw that vote even closer as the nation becomes more diverse. An American political future defined even more by racial politics is, honestly, a dystopian one in light of the nation's long and often sad history of race relations—a history that vividly reemerged during Donald Trump's racially polarizing campaign for the Republican presidential nomination in 2016. But it is a plausible one. Such a shift, however, could lead to an Electoral College in which the Midwest and the South voted the same way, a historically unlikely alliance in American presidential politics.

American presidential elections since the Civil War have featured battles between the Northeast and the South, with the two regions swapping party allegiances—the Northeast moving from Republican to Democratic and the South making the opposite shift. As long as this basic dynamic remains, it's easy to foresee Ohio, a state with both northeastern and southern-style regions, siding with one or the other in any given election, much as it has throughout its history.

The demographic argument, specifically that Ohio is whiter than the nation and therefore might become less representative, is far from preordained, in part because the white population in Ohio in 2012 was slightly less Republican than in the nation as a whole (41 percent Democratic versus 39 percent nationally). The white vote in the South has been moving toward Republicans at a much faster rate than in other regions, including the Midwest. Nate Cohn of the *New York Times*, noting the differences in political personality between white voters in the South and those elsewhere, found that Obama had "fared better than recent Democratic nominees among white voters outside the South. That's how he won battleground states like Iowa, Colorado, Wisconsin and New Hampshire."[5]

One cannot assume with complete certainty that Hispanics and Asian Americans, and even African Americans, despite having voted Democratic for so long, will invariably remain in the Democratic fold or that whites will remain as Republican as they were in those elections. Electoral coalitions change, and second- and third-generation immigrants are not necessarily bound to vote as their parents and grandparents voted. For example, just because voters of German ancestry in a place like northwest Ohio voted Democratic in the late 1800s and early 1900s does not mean that the many voters of German ancestry in these counties vote Democratic today. In fact, several of those northwest Ohio counties are now among the most Republican in the state. Parties change, ideologies change, and voters change.

Beyond demographics, though, Ohio may remain a bellwether because the state's big urban areas are increasingly coming into political alignment. Franklin is now allied with Cuyahoga as a Democratic county, and Hamilton may eventually join them. Democratic support in the state's most vote-rich counties could help counteract shifts in the suburbs and the rural parts of the state toward the Republicans. On the other hand, populations in the collar counties around Franklin and Hamilton have been growing, and they remain heavily Republican.

Yet another argument for Ohio's endurance as a bellwether through the 20th century and into the 21st is that it seemed to become an ever better reflection of national voting over time: in the 30 elections from 1896 to 2012, Ohio consistently tracked closer to the national vote in the second half of that 116-year span than in the first. From 1896 to 1952, Ohio on average deviated about three points from the national two-party vote in each election, although a few of the elections in this period (1912, 1924) had major third-party candidacies that might have skewed the two-party figures. In the second half of the period, from 1956 to 2012, Ohio on average deviated only about one point per election.

There's also not much evidence that Ohio is trending one way or the other. From 1964 through 2012—all elections in which Ohio voted for the presidential victor—these are, in order, the presidential deviations from the national two-party vote: D +2, R +1, D +1, R +1, 0, 0, R +2, R +2, R +1, R +2, 0, R +1, 0. That is, there's little indication that this slightly Republican-leaning bellwether state is moving either left or right. The only trend is that Ohio stuck close to the national average for a half century, closer even than it had in the previous half century, despite demographic trends that were much more dramatic outside the state than within it.

Still, voting trends can change in unexpected ways. Going into 2008, it would not have been obvious that Missouri, another historic bellwether, would vote against the Democratic nominee despite his comfortable win nationally. Or that West Virginia, a reliably Democratic state throughout the second half of the 20th century and a major Democratic-leaning outlier as recently as 1988, would by 2012 have one of the most pronounced Republican leans in the nation. Or that Vermont, which from 1856 to 1988 voted Democratic for president only a single time (1964), would be one of the three most-Democratic states in the 2012 election.

There are plenty of reasons to think that Ohio will remain, politically, just as it has been. But analysts must be humble in predicting the state's future and the future of the electorate as a whole.

### What Has Being a Bellwether Done for Ohio?

In 2010, the US Supreme Court opened the door to greater spending by third parties in political campaigns, leading to a flood of new groups, commonly called Super PACs. These entities can take in unlimited donations from interested donors, anonymously, and spend unlimited amounts of money on television advertising.[6]

In 2012, Les Moonves, the chief executive officer of CBS, looked ahead to the upcoming campaign and saw nothing but green: "Super PACs may be bad for America, but they're very good for CBS."[7] The more money that campaigns spend on television advertising, the more money television stations make. Although there can be many competitive statewide elections in a given year, the presidential money has become increasingly concentrated in a small number of true battleground states. Ohio is unquestionably one of them.

In a 2013 trend story about how campaign advertising boosts television station revenue in swing states, Brian Stelter of the *New York Times* observed, "For stations blessed to be in swing states, political ads routinely represent a third of their overall ad revenue in election years." WBNS, a CBS affiliate and the Columbus area's highest-rated station, grossed roughly $50 million in advertising in 2012, Stelter reported. KSTU, the highest-rated station in Salt Lake City, a similar-sized market, grossed only about $30 million in the same year. The difference, of course, is that Columbus was in a hotly contested state in the presidential race, while Salt Lake City (the capital of deeply Republican Utah) is not. Michael Fiorile, the CEO of the company that owns WBNS,[8] told Stelter that the station occasionally got complaints about the volume of campaign ads both from viewers and from nonpolitical advertisers who couldn't compete with those ads during election season. "Don't get me wrong. . . . It's a good problem for us to have," Fiorile said. "The increasingly expensive elections that play out across the country every two years are making stations look like a smart investment," Stelter wrote.[9]

In 2014, the Cincinnati-based E. W. Scripps Company and Journal Communications of Milwaukee merged, splitting off their television stations into one company and their newspapers into another. In announcing the merger, the combined company highlighted its strengthened presence in "important political states" such as Colorado, Florida, Michigan, Nevada, Ohio, and Wisconsin.[10] However, these swing-state television properties may become less valuable over time as political advertising transitions to different platforms, like cell phones and live streaming sources.

Still, at least in the short term, the consolidation of presidential elections into a select group of states has been great for the owners of television companies. It's probably not so great for most voters, including those who live in places like Democratic-leaning California and New York or Republican-leaning Texas, huge states to which presidential candidates devoted little attention in the 21st century. And it may not be great for residents of the few swing states, including the great bellwether, Ohio.

Even as the candidates vie for their attention, do Ohioans actually get anything for their trouble beyond the satisfaction, for some, of their side winning? It's hard to argue that they do, given the state's unquestionable decline through the 1970s into the 2000s and beyond.

Although Ohio's population did not actually decline in the 2010s, the state had one of the nation's slowest rates of population growth and was bleeding electoral votes (and, by extension, political power, through reduced representation in the US House) to other states. As recently as the 1960s, Ohio had 26 electoral votes; as of the 2010s, however, it had only 18.[11] That was still the seventh-highest total, so Ohio remains a prize, just not quite as big a prize as it once was.

A December 2015 census update painted a bleak picture of the state's economy. Summing up the new American Community Survey data, the *Cleveland Plain Dealer*'s Robert Higgs wrote that it showed "stagnant incomes and an increase in poverty across much of Ohio" in the first half of the 2010s.[12] Poverty was up in more than half of the state's counties, and median incomes were down in more than half of them as well. As Ohio geared up to host the Republican convention in Cleveland in 2016 and undoubtedly play a key role in that year's presidential election, it was unclear what benefit, if any, average Ohioans would get from their starring role in the proceedings.

Presidents and Congress have done little to arrest Ohio's decline. It's not their responsibility to do so to the detriment of other states—and the same population trends that have reduced the power of Ohio have affected other Rust Belt states, too—but Ohio does not receive any obviously special treatment from Washington in recognition of its bellwether status. When asked to point out any such benefits, Ohio and national political observers generally could think of only one: the big bucks that the television stations earn.

One safe political bet for 2016 and beyond, safer even than assuming that Ohio will remain among the states most crucial to winning the presidency, is that the state's value in the Electoral College will continue to fall. After the 2020 census, Ohio is projected to lose yet another electoral vote, giving the state its smallest allotment (17) since the 1820s. Perhaps the greatest long-term threat to the state's importance in presidential elections is not the growth of various minority groups in other states, but rather the greater relative growth of other states *period*, which will further reduce the Electoral College power of Ohio in the long term.

An electoral vote total in the mid-to-high teens is still quite meaningful to both parties as they attempt to cobble together Electoral College majorities. But it does lead one to wonder: if this is what happens to Ohio, which has been one of the key states—perhaps *the* key state—in electing the president for a century or more, would any other state really want the title?

# NOTES

*Introduction*

1. Richard M. Scammon and Ben J. Wattenberg, *The Real Majority: An Extraordinary Examination of the American Electorate* (New York: Coward, McCann and Geoghegan, 1970), 70.

2. Thomas Suddes, "'Typical' Buckeye Voter Is Hard to Find," *Columbus Dispatch*, July 6, 2008, http://www.dispatch.com/content/stories/editorials /2008/07/06/suddo6.ART_ART_07-06-08_E5_1FALFCQ.html.

3. "Statistics Say the 'Average Voter' Is Bette Lowrey of Ohio, But Will SHE Go Along?," *Life*, October 30, 1970, 30–32.

*Chapter 1: Swing States, Bellwethers, and the Nation's Shrinking Political Middle*

1. William M. Blair, "Missouri's Trend to GOP Watched: State, in Win Column 40 Years, May Reflect Country-Wide Sentiment, Observers Hold," *New York Times*, March 21, 1948.

2. Darshan Goux, "The Battleground State: Conceptualizing Geographic Contestation in American Presidential Elections, 1960–2004" (PhD diss., University of California, Berkeley, 2010), 17.

3. Donald Janson, "Minnesota Gives Edge to Kennedy: Humphrey Re-elected to the Senate—Governor Freeman Trailing G.O.P. Rival," *New York Times*, November 9, 1960.

4. R. W. Apple Jr., "A Guide to Things to Watch for While Following Election Returns," *New York Times*, November 2, 1976.

5. Stacey Hunter Hecht and David Schultz, "Introduction: Swing States and Presidential Elections," in *Presidential Swing States: Why Only Ten Matter*, ed. Stacey Hunter Hecht and David Schultz (Lanham, MD: Rowman and Littlefield, 2015), xi.

6. "Wave" is a commonly used term that indicates big swings in elections, but it's a term that's hard to define. Jacob Smith of the University of North Carolina came up with a good definition of a "wave election" in Congress: It is an election "that produces the potential for a political party to significantly

affect the political status quo as the result of a substantial increase in seats for that party." Jacob Smith, "Welcome to Wave Election Silly Season!," *Spes Publica* (blog), September 8, 2014, https://spespublicadotcom.wordpress.com/2014/09/08/welcome-to-wave-election-silly-season-3/.

7. Sean Trende, "The Path to the Presidency: The Past and Future Look of the Electoral College," in *The Surge: 2014's Big GOP Win and What It Means for the Next Presidential Election*, ed. Larry J. Sabato, Kyle Kondik, and Geoffrey Skelley (Lanham, MD: Rowman and Littlefield, 2015), 196–97.

8. Lynn Hudson Parsons, *The Birth of Modern Politics: Andrew Jackson, John Quincy Adams, and the Election of 1828* (New York: Oxford University Press, 2009), xvi.

9. Ibid.

10. David S. Heidler and Jeanne T. Heidler, *Henry Clay: The Essential American* (New York: Random House, 2010), 392.

11. Richard Nixon, "Speech of the Vice President at Anchorage, Alaska," November 6, 1960, The American Presidency Project, http://www.presidency.ucsb.edu/ws/index.php?pid=25324.

12. Richard Nixon, "Address Accepting the Presidential Nomination at the Republican National Convention in Chicago," July 28, 1960, The American Presidency Project, http://www.presidency.ucsb.edu/ws/?pid=25974.

13. Richard Nixon, "Speech of Vice President Richard M. Nixon, Atlanta, Georgia," August 26, 1960, The American Presidency Project, http://www.presidency.ucsb.edu/ws/index.php?pid=25463.

14. Richard Nixon, "Partial Transcript of Remarks by the Vice President, Memorial Auditorium, Burlington, VT," September 29, 1960, The American Presidency Project, http://www.presidency.ucsb.edu/ws/index.php?pid=25505.

15. Theodore White, *The Making of the President 1960* (New York: Atheneum, 1961), 267.

16. Larry J. Sabato, *The Kennedy Half-Century: The Presidency, Assassination, and Lasting Legacy of John F. Kennedy* (New York: Bloomsbury, 2013), 70.

17. Miller Center of Public Affairs, University of Virginia, "Dwight D. Eisenhower: Campaigns and Elections," http://millercenter.org/president/biography/eisenhower-campaigns-and-elections.

18. R. Hal Williams, *Realigning America: McKinley, Bryan, and the Remarkable Election of 1896* (Lawrence: University Press of Kansas, 2010), 99.

19. Richard J. Ellis and Mark Dedrick, "The Presidential Candidate, Then and Now," *Perspectives on Political Science* 26, no. 4 (Fall 1997): 208–16.

20. Presidential deviation is a modified version of the *Cook Political Report*'s Partisan Voter Index, which the respected national political hand-icapping newsletter uses to measure how congressional districts perform at the presidential level. This book uses the term *presidential deviation* be-cause it and PVI are slightly different. Presidential deviation measures the performance of a county or state against the presidential result in a given year, while PVI measures the performance of a congressional district by averaging its presidential performance in the two most recent elections.

21. Bill Bishop, *The Big Sort: Why the Clustering of Like-Minded America Is Tearing Us Apart* (New York: Mariner, 2009), 14.

22. The list of counties defined as Appalachian by the Appala-chian Regional Commission is available at http://www.arc.gov/research /MapsofAppalachia.asp?MAP_ID=31. It's a big region, extending all the way from western New York to northern Alabama and Mississippi.

23. Edison Research, "Exit Poll for Presidential Race," November 6, 2012, http://www.cbsnews.com/election-results-2012/exit.shtml?state=US&race =P&jurisdiction=0&party=G&tag=contentBody;exitLink.

24. Alan Abramowitz and Steven Webster, "All Politics Is National: The Rise of Negative Partisanship and the Nationalization of U.S. House and Senate Elections in the 21st Century," paper presented at the Annual Meeting of the Midwest Political Science Association, Chicago, Illinois, April 16–19, 2015, http://www.stevenwwebster.com/research/all_politics_is _national.pdf.

25. American Enterprise Institute and Brookings Institution, "Table 2-16: Ticket Splitting between Presidential and House Candidates, 1900–2012," *Vital Statistics on Congress*, August 2014, http://www.brookings.edu/~/media /Research/Files/Reports/2013/07/vital-statistics-congress-mann-ornstein /Vital-Statistics-Chapter-2--Congressional-Elections.pdf?la=en.

26. Brendan Nyhan, "Missing Context on Growth in Polarization," Decem-ber 28, 2009, http://www.brendan-nyhan.com/blog/2009/12/missing-context -on-growth-in-polarization.html.

27. Center for Voting and Democracy, "Presidential Tracker," http://www .fairvote.org/presidential_elections#presidential_tracker.

*Chapter 2: Ohio at the Head of the Flock*

1. "General Election: Romney vs. Obama," RealClearPolitics, http://www .realclearpolitics.com/epolls/2012/president/us/general_election_romney _vs_obama-1171.html.

2. Gallup, "U.S. Presidential Election Center," http://www.gallup.com/poll/154559/US-Presidential-Election-Center.aspx?ref=interactive.

3. "Battleground State Polls," RealClearPolitics, http://www.realclearpolitics.com/epolls/2012/president/battleground_states.html.

4. V. O. Key, Jr., "A Theory of Critical Elections," *Journal of Politics* 17, no. 1 (February 1955): 3–18, http://faculty.smu.edu/jmwilson/Key1.pdf.

5. John Gerring, *Party Ideologies in America: 1828–1996* (New York: Cambridge University Press, 1998).

6. Kyle Kondik, "Ohio, New Mexico the Best Presidential Bellwethers," *Sabato's Crystal Ball*, June 11, 2015, http://www.centerforpolitics.org/crystalball/articles/ohio-new-mexico-the-best-presidential-bellwethers/.

7. Sean Trende, *The Lost Majority: Why the Future of Government Is Up for Grabs—and Who Will Take It* (New York: Palgrave Macmillan, 2012).

8. Sean Trende, "As Goes Washington, So Goes the Nation," RealClearPolitics, August 18, 2010, http://www.realclearpolitics.com/articles/2010/08/18/as_goes_washington_so_goes_the_nation_106799.html.

9. Howard Berkes, "What Is An Election Bellwether?," NPR, October 24, 2008, http://www.npr.org/templates/story/story.php?storyId=96116110.

10. "The Bellwether," *Economist*, June 3, 2004, http://www.economist.com/node/2733358.

11. There was something symbolic about the state's flagship university, the University of Missouri, joining the Southeastern Conference in athletics starting in 2012. It was previously part of the Big 12, which includes universities in the Great Plains as well as Texas, while the SEC includes the flagship universities of many southern states.

12. Edison Research, "New Mexico Exit Poll for Presidential Race," November 6, 2012, http://www.cbsnews.com/election-results-2012/exit.shtml?state=NM&race=P&jurisdiction=0&party=G&tag=dataDisplay;2823.

13. Stephen Henderson, "State Voting History. The Most Accurate Bellwether[:] You'd Never Guess Which State Predicted the Most 20th Century Presidents," *Chicago Tribune*, October 14, 1996, http://articles.chicagotribune.com/1996-10-14/news/9701150365_1_bellwether-new-mexico-midwest-states.

14. Jon Ralston, personal correspondence with author, July 30, 2015.

15. Edison Research, "Nevada Exit Poll for Presidential Race," November 6, 2012, http://www.cbsnews.com/election-results-2012/exit.shtml?state=NV&race=P&jurisdiction=0&party=G&tag=dataDisplay;2835.

1. Harlan Hatcher, *The Buckeye Country: A Pageant of Ohio* (New York: H. C. Kinsey, 1940), 311.

2. Daniel J. Coffey, John C. Green, David B. Cohen, and Stephen C. Brooks, *Buckeye Battleground: Ohio, Campaigns, and Elections in the Twenty-First Century* (Akron: University of Akron Press, 2011), 35.

3. Kevin F. Kern and Gregory S. Wilson, *Ohio: A History of the Buckeye State* (Chichester, UK: John Wiley, 2014), 112.

4. George W. Knepper, *Ohio and Its People*, 3rd ed. (Kent, OH: Kent State University Press, 2003), 49.

5. Ibid., 48.

6. Kern and Wilson, *Ohio: A History of the Buckeye State*, 133–34.

7. Ibid.

8. Colin Woodard, *American Nations: A History of the Eleven Rival Regional Cultures of North America* (New York: Viking Penguin, 2011), 7.

9. Kern and Wilson, *Ohio: A History of the Buckeye State*, 248.

10. D. W. Meinig, *The Shaping of America: A Geographical Perspective on 500 Years of History*, vol. 2, *Continental America 1800–1867* (New Haven: Yale University Press, 1993), 281–82.

11. Ohio State Archaeological and Historical Society, *The Ohio Guide* (American Guide Series) (New York: Oxford University Press, 1943), 16.

12. "Ohio's Centennial Celebration," *Editorial Review*, July 1912, 651, available at https://books.google.com/books?id=knhHAAAAYAAJ.

13. Mike Dawson, "Ohio President Region Results Combined 2012–1856," http://ohioelectionresults.com/documents/Presidential/Ohio%20President%20Region%202012–1856.pdf.

14. Woodard, *American Nations*, 13.

15. John Fenton, *Midwest Politics* (New York: Holt, Rinehart and Winston, 1966), 117.

16. Brandon Rottinghaus and Justin S. Vaughn, "Measuring Obama against the Great Presidents," *FixGov* (blog), Brookings Institution, February 13, 2015, http://www.brookings.edu/blogs/fixgov/posts/2015/02/13-obama-measuring-presidential-greatness-vaughn-rottinghaus.

17. Richard G. Zimmerman, "Rhodes's First Eight Years, 1963–1971," in *Ohio Politics*, rev. ed., ed. Alexander P. Lamis and Brian Usher (Kent, OH: Kent State University Press, 2007), 91.

18. Tom Suddes, "A Riff on Kasich's Budget," *Columbus Monthly*, June 2011, http://www.columbusmonthly.com/content/stories/2011/06/a-riff-on-kasich039s-budget.html.

19. Geoffrey Skelley, "Coattails and Correlation: Presidential and Senate Results Should Track Closely in 2016—and That's Nothing New," *Sabato's Crystal Ball*, March 5, 2015, http://www.centerforpolitics.org/crystalball/articles/coattails-and-correlation-examining-the-relationship-between-presidential-and-senate-results/.

20. Gerald M. Pomper, ed., *The Election of 1988: Reports and Interpretations* (Chatham, NJ: Chatham House, 1989), 166–67.

21. Bernard Weinraub, "Ray C. Bliss Dies in Ohio at 73, Rebuilt G.O.P. After 1964 Rout," *New York Times*, August 7, 1981, http://www.nytimes.com/1981/08/07/obituaries/ray-c-bliss-dies-in-ohio-at-73-rebuilt-gop-after-1964-rout.html

22. Betsy Klein, "Donald Trump Retweet Cites Iowans' 'Issues in the Brain,'" CNN, October 22, 2015, http://www.cnn.com/2015/10/22/politics/donald-trump-iowa-retweet/.

23. Scott Neuman, "Trump Lashes Out at McCain: 'I Like People Who Weren't Captured,'" NPR, July 18, 2015, http://www.npr.org/sections/thetwo-way/2015/07/18/424169549/trump-lashes-out-at-mccain-i-like-people-who-werent-captured.

24. Paul Solotaroff, "Trump Seriously: On the Trail With the GOP's Tough Guy," *Rolling Stone*, September 9, 2015, http://www.rollingstone.com/politics/news/trump-seriously-20150909.

25. Daniel Lathrop, "Iowa Isn't the State Presidential Candidates Pretend It Is," *FiveThirtyEight*, December 14, 2015, http://fivethirtyeight.com/features/iowa-isnt-the-state-presidential-candidates-pretend-it-is/.

26. "The Midwest," *Washington Post*, November 10, 1988, https://www.washingtonpost.com/archive/politics/1988/11/10/the-midwest/bb9e387f-1bb2-4f14-b8df-75d654e88ee3/.

27. Tom Feran, "John Kasich Says Agriculture Is the 'Strongest Industry in Ohio,'" PolitiFact Ohio, December 12, 2012, http://www.politifact.com/ohio/statements/2012/dec/12/john-kasich/john-kasich-says-agriculture-strongest-industry-oh/.

28. Tracy Smith, "Columbus, Ohio: Test Market of the U.S.A.," CBS News, June 24, 2012, http://www.cbsnews.com/news/columbus-ohio-test-market-of-the-usa/.

29. Knepper, *Ohio and Its People*, xi.

1. Eugene H. Roseboom, *The History of the State of Ohio*, vol. 4, *The Civil War Era 1850–1873* (Columbus: Ohio State Archaeological and Historical Society, 1944), 409.

2. Ibid., 406.

3. Ibid., 411.

4. James M. McPherson, *Tried by War: Abraham Lincoln as Commander in Chief* (New York: Penguin, 2008), 172.

5. George W. Knepper, *Ohio and Its People*, 3rd ed. (Kent, OH: Kent State University Press, 2003), 232, 236.

6. Vallandigham died, ignominiously, in 1871. Vallandigham was defending a man accused of a shooting. He tried to show a friend how the gun could fire accidentally and, in so doing, accidentally shot and killed himself.

7. Kevin Phillips, *The Emerging Republican Majority* (1969; repr., Princeton: Princeton University Press, 2015), 345, 377.

8. The only other county with a black population over 10 percent was Salem County, New Jersey, which lies across the Delaware River from Delaware, which was a slave state until the end of the Civil War. (New Jersey itself was a slave state in its early days of statehood but outlawed the practice in 1804.)

9. William T. Horner, *Ohio's Kingmaker: Mark Hanna, Man and Myth* (Athens: Ohio University Press, 2010), 266.

10. Arthur Sears Henning, "Northern Ohio Turns to Wilson on Single Issue," *Chicago Daily Tribune*, October 19, 1916, http://archives.chicagotribune .com/1916/10/19/page/7/article/northern-ohio-turns-to-wilson-on-single -issue.

11. John Milton Cooper Jr., *Woodrow Wilson: A Biography* (New York: Alfred A. Knopf, 2009), 359.

12. Ibid., 447.

13. "Ake Law," Ohio History Connection, http://www.ohiohistorycentral .org/w/Ake_Law.

14. "The Gender Gap: Voting Choices in Presidential Elections," Center for the American Woman and Politics, December 2012, http://www.cawp .rutgers.edu/sites/default/files/resources/ggpresvote.pdf.

15. Steven J. Rosenstone, Roy L. Behr, and Edward H. Lazarus, *Third Parties in America: Citizen Response to Major Party Failure*, 2nd ed. (Princeton: Princeton University Press, 1996), 95.

16. Phillips, *The Emerging Republican Majority*, 386.

17. Michael Barone, *Shaping Our Nation: How Surges of Migration Transformed America and Its Politics* (New York: Crown Forum, 2013), 145.

18. Kevin F. Kern and Gregory S. Wilson, *Ohio: A History of the Buckeye State* (Chichester, UK: John Wiley, 2014), 369.

19. Robert A. Taft, *The Papers of Robert A. Taft*, vol. 1, *1889–1938*, ed. Clarence E. Wunderlin, Jr. (Kent, OH: Kent State University Press, 1997), 304.

20. Thomas Suddes, "Newton D. Baker: Cleveland's Greatest Mayor," Teaching Cleveland, http://www.teachingcleveland.org/index.php?option=com_k2&view=item&id=868:newton-d-baker-cleveland%E2%80%99s-greatest-mayor-by-thomas-suddes.

21. Thomas A. Flinn, "Continuity and Change in Ohio Politics," *Journal of Politics* 24, no. 3 (August 1962): 521–44, http://www.jstor.org/stable/2127705.

22. Nancy J. Weiss, *Farewell to the Party of Lincoln: Black Politics in the Age of FDR* (Princeton: Princeton University Press, 1983), 206.

*Chapter 5: Roosevelt, Eisenhower, and Nixon—but Not Taft, 1936–1972*

1. David M. Kennedy, *Freedom from Fear: The American People in Depression and War, 1929–1945* (New York: Oxford University Press, 1999), 286.

2. Nancy J. Weiss, *Farewell to the Party of Lincoln: Black Politics in the Age of FDR* (Princeton: Princeton University Press, 1983), 206.

3. Ibid., 212.

4. This is based on two-party presidential deviation by county. The 17 counties that had Democratic-leaning deviations in 1932 and then have had Republican deviations in every election since are Allen, Ashland, Auglaize, Clermont, Darke, Fairfield, Fayette, Hardin, Henry, Marion, Paulding, Preble, Seneca, Van Wert, Washington, Williams, and Wyandot. The five others with just an exception or two since 1932 are Coshocton, Crawford, Defiance, Putnam, and Ross.

5. Michael Barone, *Our Country: The Shaping of America from Roosevelt to Reagan* (New York: Free Press, 1990), 105.

6. James T. Patterson, *Mr. Republican: A Biography of Robert A. Taft* (Boston: Houghton Mifflin Company, 1972), 213, 216–19.

7. Robert A. Taft, *The Papers of Robert A. Taft*, vol. 2, *1939–1944*, ed. Clarence E. Wunderlin Jr. (Kent, OH: Kent State University Press, 2001), 160.

8. Samuel Lubell, "Post-Mortem: Who Elected Roosevelt?," *Saturday Evening Post*, January 25, 1941, 9.

9. Bernard Sternsher, "The Harding and Bricker Revolutions: Party Systems and Voter Behavior in Northwest Ohio, 1860–1982," *Northwest Ohio Quarterly* 59, no. 3 (Summer 1987), 91–118.

10. Susan Dunn, *1940: FDR, Willkie, Lindbergh, Hitler—the Election amid the Storm* (New Haven: Yale University Press, 2013), 264.

11. Andrew Cayton, *Ohio: The History of a People* (Columbus: Ohio State University Press, 2002), 324.

12. "Man in the News," *New York Times,* November 5, 1964, http://www.nytimes.com/1964/11/05/man-in-the-news.html?_r=0.

13. John Gunther, *Inside U.S.A.* (New York: Harper and Brothers, 1946), 436.

14. John Sides, "Seven Questions about the 2012 Campaign," *The Monkey Cage* (blog), July 29, 2012, http://themonkeycage.org/2012/07/seven-questions-about-the-2012-campaign/.

15. Robert L. Dudley and Ronald B. Rapoport, "Vice-Presidential Candidates and the Home State Advantage: Playing Second Banana at Home and on the Road," *American Journal of Political Science* 33, no. 2 (May 1989): 537–40, http://www.jstor.org/stable/2111159.

16. Nate Silver, "The Overrated Vice-Presidential Home State Effect," *New York Times,* April 23, 2012, http://fivethirtyeight.blogs.nytimes.com/2012/04/23/the-overrated-vice-presidential-home-state-effect/.

17. George W. Knepper, *Ohio and Its People,* 3rd ed. (Kent, OH: Kent State University Press, 2003), 375.

18. Donald S. Inbody, *The Soldier Vote: War, Politics, and the Ballot in America* (New York: Palgrave Macmillan, 2015), 8.

19. Ira Katznelson, *Fear Itself: The New Deal and the Origins of Our Time* (New York: Liveright, 2013), 215–22.

20. Patterson, *Mr. Republican,* 415.

21. Raymond Moley, "Raymond Moley Predicts Landslide for Tom Dewey," *Spokane Daily Chronicle,* November 1, 1948, https://news.google.com/newspapers?id=MagVAAAAIBAJ&sjid=v_UDAAAAIBAJ&pg=3420%2C180861.

22. Samuel Lubell, *The Future of American Politics* (New York: Harper and Brothers, 1952), 134.

23. Ibid., 211.

24. Patterson, *Mr. Republican,* 425–26.

25. Richard G. Zimmerman, "Rhodes's First Eight Years, 1963–1971," in *Ohio Politics,* rev. ed., ed. Alexander P. Lamis and Brian Usher (Kent, OH: Kent State University Press, 2007), 89.

26. Thomas Suddes, "Ohio Needs More Officials Who Fight For the Little Guy," *Columbus Dispatch,* May 10, 2015, http://www.dispatch.com /content/stories/editorials/2015/05/10/1-ohio-needs-more-officials-who -fight-for-the-little-guy.html.

27. Samuel Lubell, "How Taft Did It," *Saturday Evening Post,* February 10, 1951, 32.

28. Robert A. Taft, *The Papers of Robert A. Taft,* vol. 4, *1949–1953,* ed. Clarence E. Wunderlin Jr. (Kent, OH: Kent State University Press, 2006), 395.

29. Taft, *The Papers of Robert A. Taft,* vol. 2, *1939–1944,* 245.

30. Robert A. Taft, "How I Lost the Nomination," *Human Events,* December 2, 1959.

31. David Halberstam, *The Powers That Be* (1979; repr., Chicago: University of Illinois Press, 2000), 92.

32. Thomas Suddes, "Nixon's Political, Family Ties to Ohio Remembered," *Cleveland Plain Dealer,* April 23, 1994, 6A.

33. Richard Nixon, "Remarks of the Vice President, Rear Train Platform, Athens, OH," October 25, 1960, The American Presidency Project, http:// www.presidency.ucsb.edu/ws/index.php?pid=25454.

34. "Election Polls—Vote by Groups, 1960–1964," Gallup, http://www .gallup.com/poll/9454/election-polls-vote-groups-19601964.aspx.

35. Thomas A. Flinn, "How Mr. Nixon Took Ohio: A Short Reply to Senator Kennedy's Question," *Western Political Quarterly* 15, no. 2 (June 1962): 274–79.

36. André Bernard and Clifton Fadiman, *Bartlett's Book of Anecdotes,* rev. ed. (Boston: Little Brown and Company, 2000), 317.

37. Tom Diemer, Lee Leonard, and Richard G. Zimmerman, *James A. Rhodes, Ohio Colossus* (Kent, OH: Kent State University Press, 2014), 45.

38. Zimmerman, "Rhodes's First Eight Years, 1963–1971," 103.

39. Tom Reynders, "Wallace Backers In Ohio Plan To Go For Broke," *Toledo Blade,* September 27, 1968, https://news.google.com/newspapers ?nid=1350&dat=19680926&id=ccZOAAAAIBAJ&sjid=oAEEAAAAIBAJ &pg=2864,3990404&hl=en.

40. Williams v. Rhodes, 393 U.S. 23 (1968), https://supreme.justia.com /cases/federal/us/393/23/.

41. The eight counties wholly contained within the Virginia Military District are Adams, Brown, Clermont, Clinton, Fayette, Highland, Madison, and Union.

42. William K. Stevens, "In Ohio 'Melting Pot' Ward, the Election Is Far Away," *New York Times,* February 14, 1976, http://query.nytimes.com/mem /archive-free/pdf?res=9E05E3DE1E30E036A05757C1A9649C946790D6CF.

43. James T. Patterson, *Grand Expectations: The United States, 1945–1974* (New York: Oxford University Press, 1996), 705.

44. Kevin F. Kern and Gregory S. Wilson, *Ohio: A History of the Buckeye State* (Chichester, UK: John Wiley, 2014), 453.

45. Zimmerman, "Rhodes's First Eight Years, 1963–1971," 107.

*Chapter 6: Obama Rewrites the Carter-Clinton Playbook, 1976–2012*

1. R. W. Apple Jr., "Carter and Ford in a Tight Race in Midwest, With Ohio Key State," *New York Times*, October 22, 1976, http://query.nytimes.com/mem /archive-free/pdf?res=950DEEDD113AE03BBC4A51DFB667838D669EDE.

2. Henry Howe, *Historical Collections of Ohio*, vol. 2 (Norwalk, OH: State of Ohio/Laning Printing Company, 1896), 268.

3. Kevin Phillips, *American Political Report* 6, no. 10, February 4, 1977.

4. The 15 "collar counties" are Geauga, Lake, Lorain, Medina, Portage, and Summit around Cuyahoga; Delaware, Fairfield, Licking, Madison, Pickaway, and Union around Franklin; and Butler, Clermont, and Warren around Hamilton.

5. Phil Gailey, "The Nation: Hart Exit Changes Rules; Searching for a New Face," *New York Times*, June 7, 1987, http://www.nytimes.com/1987/06/07 /weekinreview/the-nation-hart-exit-changes-rules-serching-for-a-new-face.html.

6. "Samuel P. Bush, 83, a Steel Executive," *New York Times*, February 9, 1948, http://query.nytimes.com/mem/archive/pdf?res=9E0DE4D71530E23 ABC4153DFB4668383659EDE.

7. Presidential Job Approval Center, Gallup, http://www.gallup.com/poll /124922/presidential-job-approval-center.aspx.

8. John B. Judis, "The Return of the Middle American Radical," *National Journal*, October 2, 2015, http://www.nationaljournal.com/s/74221 /return-middle-american-radical.

9. Steven A. Holmes, "The 1992 Elections: Disappointment—News Analysis: An Eccentric but No Joke; Perot's Strong Showing Raises Questions On What Might Have Been, and Might Be," *New York Times*, November 5, 1992, http://www.nytimes.com/1992/11/05/us/1992-elections -disappointment-analysis-eccentric-but-no-joke-perot-s-strong.html.

10. Perot's best 15 counties in Ohio were, in alphabetical order: Carroll, Columbiana, Crawford, Hocking, Huron, Medina, Mercer, Morrow, Paulding, Perry, Portage, Seneca, Shelby, Williams, and Wyandot.

11. E. J. Dionne Jr., "Perot Seen Not Affecting Vote Outcome," *Washington Post*, November 8, 1992, https://www.washingtonpost.com/archive

/politics/1992/11/08/perot-seen-not-affecting-vote-outcome/27500538-cee8 -4f4f-8e7f-f3ee9f2325d1/.

12. Ibid.

13. Michael F. Curtin and Joe Hallett, *The Ohio Politics Almanac*, 3rd rev. ed. (Kent, OH: Kent State University Press, 2015), 207.

14. Larry J. Sabato, Kyle Kondik, and Geoffrey Skelley, "12 From '12: Some Takeaways from a Wild Election," *Sabato's Crystal Ball*, November 15, 2012, http://www.centerforpolitics.org/crystalball/articles/12-from-12-some -takeaways-from-a-wild-election/.

15. The exceptions were Belmont, Clark, Hamilton, Jefferson, Lake, Monroe, Ottawa, Sandusky, Stark, Tuscarawas, and Wood. Of those, the three that cast more than 100,000 votes in 2012 were Hamilton (418,894), Stark (181,746), and Lake (118,665).

16. The Public Religion Research Institute's Dan Cox performed this analysis of PRRI polling data for the author.

17. The exception was Mercer, a heavily Catholic county located on the Indiana border.

18. Farhad Manjoo, "Was the 2004 Election Stolen? No.," *Salon*, June 3, 2006, http://www.salon.com/2006/06/03/kennedy_39/.

19. Thomas Suddes, "Anti-Gay Issue Didn't Save Bush," *Cleveland Plain Dealer*, December 30, 2007, M1.

20. Richard Morin and Claudia Deane, "Report Acknowledges Inaccuracies in 2004 Exit Polls," *Washington Post*, January 20, 2005, http://www .washingtonpost.com/wp-dyn/articles/A22188-2005Jan19.html?nav =rss_politics/elections/2004.

21. "Ohio 2004 Polls," RealClearPolitics, http://www.realclearpolitics .com/Presidential_04/oh_polls.html.

22. "Conspiracy Theories Prosper: 25% of Americans Are 'Truthers,'" Fairleigh Dickinson University's PublicMind Poll, January 17, 2013, http:// publicmind.fdu.edu/2013/outthere/.

23. Jim DeBrosse, Lawrence Budd, and Ken McCall, "Moral Issues Swung for Bush," *Dayton Daily News*, November 7, 2004, 1A.

24. Adam Nagourney, "'Moral Values' Carried Bush, Rove Says," *New York Times*, November 10, 2004, http://www.nytimes.com/2004/11/10/politics /campaign/moral-values-carried-bush-rove-says.html. It is amazing that less than a dozen years later, in 2015, the Supreme Court would mandate same-sex marriage be legal in all 50 states.

25. Paul Taylor, "Wedge Issues on the Ballot," Pew Research Center, July 26, 2006, http://www.pewresearch.org/2006/07/26/wedge-issues-on-the-ballot/.

26. In unpublished research, Henry Olsen of the Ethics and Public Policy Center studied heavy African American areas in Ohio and determined that the exit poll overstated black support for Bush in 2004 (interview with the author, January 29, 2016).

27. Daniel A. Smith, Matt DeSantis, and Jason Kassel, "Was Rove Right? Evangelicals and the Impact of Gay Marriage in the 2004 Election," paper presented at the 5th Annual State Politics and Policy Conference, May 12–14, 2005, at Michigan State University, http://polisci.msu.edu/sppc2005/papers /fripm/Smith%20DeSantis%20Kassel%20Was%20Rove%20Right.pdf.

28. David E. Campbell and J. Quin Monson, "The Religion Card: Gay Marriage and the 2004 Presidential Election," *Public Opinion Quarterly* 72, no. 3 (Fall 2008), 399–419, http://www.jstor.org/stable/pdf/25167637.

29. The eight southwest Ohio counties, as defined by the *Ohio Politics Almanac*, are Adams, Brown, Butler, Clermont, Clinton, Hamilton, Highland, and Warren.

30. Mark Blumenthal, "Obama Campaign Polls: How the Internal Data Got It Right," *HuffPost Pollster*, November 21, 2012, http://www.huffingtonpost .com/2012/11/21/obama-campaign-polls-2012_n_2171242.html.

31. Brent Larkin, "Surge of Black Votes Wasn't Romney's Undoing," *Cleveland Plain Dealer*, March 9, 2013, http://www.cleveland.com/opinion /index.ssf/2013/03/surge_of_black_votes_wasnt_rom.html.

*Chapter 7: Searching for the Bellwether's Bellwether*

1. Everett C. Ladd, "Magic Town: Jimmy Stewart Demonstrates the 'Hawthorne Effect,'" *Public Perspective* 7, no. 3 (April–May 1996): 16–17, https://ropercenter.cornell.edu/public-perspective/ppscan/73/73016.pdf.

2. Susan Q. Stranahan, "Summer Infestation Descends upon Canton, Ohio," *Columbia Journalism Review*, July 2, 2004, http://www.cjr.org/politics /summer_infestation_descends_up.php?nomobile=1.

3. Peronet Despeignes, "Brits' campaign backfires in Ohio," *USA Today*, November 4, 2004, http://usatoday30.usatoday.com/news/politicselections /vote2004/2004-11-04-brits-letters_x.htm.

4. George Gallup, "Ohio County Prophet Gives F.D.R. Majority," *Cleveland Plain Dealer*, August 21, 1938, 1A.

5. Paul F. Lazarsfeld, Bernard R. Berelson, and Hazel Gaudet, *The People's Choice: How the Voter Makes Up His Mind in a Presidential Campaign* (New York: Duell, Sloan and Pearce, 1944), 3.

6. Sparsely populated Summit, Utah, did vote for the winner in 1940, but then voted for the losing candidate in 1948.

7. Edward R. Tufte and Richard A. Sun, "Are There Bellwether Electoral Districts?," *Public Opinion Quarterly* 39, no. 1 (Spring 1975): 1–18, http://www.edwardtufte.com/files/Bellwether3.pdf.

8. Daniel J. Coffey, "The Myth of the Ohio Bellwether County," University of Akron Ray C. Bliss Institute of Applied Politics, https://www.uakron.edu/dotAsset/6b5ef655-447c-4a73-90d4-f2eb46ca7ffd.pdf.

9. David Murphy, "Obama Won a Record-Low Share of U.S. Counties—But He Won Them Big," NBCNews.com, December 4, 2012, http://www.nbcnews.com/id/50073771/t/obama-won-record-low-share-us-counties-he-won-them-big/#.VpQmt_krJD8.

10. The city of Sandusky is not actually in Sandusky County. It is in Erie County.

11. Dick Kimmins, "Big-County Tallies Hurt Gorman Bid," *Cincinnati Enquirer*, November 5, 1992, B3.

12. The exceptions are as follows, with the years they voted Democratic in parentheses: Adams (1976), Brown (1976), Carroll (1992, 1996), Coshocton (1992), Gallia (1996), Guernsey (1992, 1996), Huron (1996), Jackson (1976, 1996), Lawrence (1976, 1992, 1976), Meigs (1976, 1992, 1996), Mercer (1968), Noble (1996), Seneca (1996), and Vinton (1976, 1992, 1996).

13. Nearly all of Columbus is in Franklin County, but small parts of it reach into Delaware and Fairfield Counties as well.

14. "American Values Atlas, Public Religion Research Institute, http://ava.publicreligion.org/#religious/2014/MetroAreas/religion/m/5,6,7.

15. "Exit Poll for Presidential Race," Edison Research, November 6, 2012, http://www.cbsnews.com/election-results-2012/exit.shtml?state=US&race=P&jurisdiction=0&party=G&tag=contentBody;exitLink.

16. Those are, in order of highest-to-lowest incomes, Delaware, Warren, Geauga, Medina, Union, Putnam, Fairfield, Clermont, Greene, and Butler.

*Conclusion: Will Ohio Remain a Bellwether (and Will It Lose Anything If It Doesn't)?*

1. Joe Hallett, "Both Major Parties Are Distracted by Internal Battles," *Columbus Dispatch*, April 1, 2012, http://www.dispatch.com/content/stories/editorials/2012/04/01/both-major-ohio-parties-are-distracted-by-internal-battles.html.

2. Nate Silver, "There's Nothing Special about Ohio," *New York Times*, March 9, 2011, http://fivethirtyeight.blogs.nytimes.com/2011/03/09/theres-nothing-special-about-ohio/?_r=0.

3. Alfred J. Tuchfarber, "Ohio: Presidential Politics in 'The Heart of It All,'" *Rothenberg Political Report* 5, no. 1 (Winter 1987–88): 15–18.

4. Gregor Aisch, Robert Gebeloff, and Kevin Quealy, "Where We Came From and Where We Went, State by State," *The Upshot*, updated August 19, 2014, http://www.nytimes.com/interactive/2014/08/13/upshot/where-people-in-each-state-were-born.html.

5. Nate Cohn, "Southern Whites' Loyalty to G.O.P. Nearing That of Blacks to Democrats," *New York Times*, April 23, 2014, http://www.nytimes.com/2014/04/24/upshot/southern-whites-loyalty-to-gop-nearing-that-of-blacks-to-democrats.html.

6. In practice, though, Super PACs are not as efficient as traditional candidate spending. Candidates get better rates for television advertising than outside groups do, making the candidates' dollars go further.

7. Andy Fixmer, "CBS Profit to Climb $180 Million on Political Ads, CEO Says," *Bloomberg*, March 10, 2012, http://www.bloomberg.com/news/articles/2012-03-10/political-tv-ads-on-cbs-will-increase-profit-by-180-million-moonves-says.

8. The Dispatch Broadcast Group owns WBNS. The broadcast group is owned by the Wolfe family, who until 2015 owned the *Columbus Dispatch*, the capital city's only major newspaper.

9. Brian Stelter, "Campaign Ad Cash Lures Buyers to Swing-State TV Stations," *New York Times*, July 7, 2013, http://www.nytimes.com/2013/07/08/business/media/with-political-ad-profits-swing-state-tv-stations-are-hot-properties.html.

10. "Scripps, Journal Merging Broadcast Operations, Spinning Off Newspapers," Journal Communications press release, July 30, 2014, http://phx.corporate-ir.net/phoenix.zhtml?c=145779&p=irol-newsArticle&ID=1953344.

11. A state's electoral votes represent its apportionment of members of Congress, which is based on population. The bigger a state's population, the more House members it has. There are 435 House members, and 538 total electoral votes: The extra 103 electoral votes represent the 100 members of the US Senate (two per state, so the lowest number of electoral votes any state can have is three) and three electoral votes for the District of Columbia, which has a say in presidential elections but does not actually have two senators or a voting member of the US House.

12. Robert Higgs, "Ohio Incomes Flat, Poverty up over Last Five Years, Census Snapshot Shows," *Cleveland Plain Dealer*, December 10, 2015, http://www.cleveland.com/metro/index.ssf/2015/12/ohio_incomes_flat_poverty_up_0.html.

# A Note on Sources

Presidential election results from the United States, Ohio, and Ohio's counties used throughout this book are almost exclusively taken from Dave Leip's Atlas of U.S. Presidential Elections website (http://uselectionatlas .org/). It is an excellent site frequently used by election analysts and researchers. Ohio regional voting patterns, non-presidential results, and selected county-level Ohio results not available on Dave Leip's site (the year 1900 in particular) are from the Ohio Historical Election Results site (http://ohioelectionresults.com/) maintained by Mike Dawson. Some of the maps from this site are used in this book, and Mike's site is an incredible resource that one can only hope enterprising people in other states will mimic. Historical election results at the city and precinct levels reported throughout the book are generally from secondary sources, although results from 21st-century elections at those smaller levels of analysis are from the Ohio Secretary of State's office and county boards of elections.

Another excellent resource for election results and for Ohio political history is the *Ohio Politics Almanac* (2015) by Mike Curtin and Joe Hallett. *Buckeye Battleground: Ohio, Campaigns, and Elections in the Twenty-First Century* (2011) by Daniel J. Coffey, John C. Green, David B. Cohen, and Stephen C. Brooks of the University of Akron's Ray C. Bliss Institute of Applied Politics provides a detailed analysis of Ohio's voting in the 21st century's first decade.

Some of the finest analyses of Ohio election results and trends comes from sources released in the 1940s, 1950s, and 1960s. Two academic articles from Thomas A. Flinn help describe the state's presidential voting patterns: "The Outline of Ohio Politics" (1960) and "Continuity and Change in Ohio Politics" (1962). Another Flinn article, "How Mr. Nixon Took Ohio: A Short Reply to Senator Kennedy's Question" (1962), shows how religious voting colored the 1960 race, a contest worth exploring in detail given that 1960 was one of only two times from 1896 to 2012 (1944 was the other) that Ohio did not vote for the presidential winner. Samuel Lubell's writings from the *Saturday Evening Post* after the elections of 1940 ("Post-Mortem: Who Elected Roosevelt?") and 1948 ("Who Really Elected Truman?") and Senator Robert A. Taft's midterm reelection in 1950 ("How Taft Did It") provide rich accounts of Ohio's voting habits at the middle of the 20th century, as does Lubell's book *The Future of American Politics* (1952). John H. Fenton's *Midwest Politics* (1966) places Ohio in the context of its midwestern neighbors and describes its "issue-less" politics. Kevin Phillips's *The Emerging Republican Majority* (1969) remains an incredible work for its rich descriptions of voting patterns both in Ohio and in the nation as a whole.

Bernard Sternsher's articles from 1987, "The Harding and Bricker Revolutions: Party Systems and Voter Behavior in Northwest Ohio," and 1990, "The Glenn Revolution: Voter Behavior in Northwest Ohio," describe how the state's northwestern region's political tendencies evolved over time.

*Ohio Politics* (2007), edited by Alexander Lamis and Brian Usher, features essays from many Ohio political experts, mostly focused on state-level politics and politicians of the second half of the 20th century. John J. Gargan and James G. Coke's *Political Behavior and Public Issues in Ohio* (1972) and Paul Sracic and William Binning's *Ohio Government and Politics* (2016) explain Ohio political history, voting patterns, and state governmental structures. Three major histories of Ohio are *Ohio and Its People* (2003) by George Knepper, *Ohio: The History of a People* (2002) by Andrew R. L. Cayton, and *Ohio: A History of the Buckeye State* (2014) by Kevin F. Kern and Gregory S. Wilson. *The Geography of Ohio* (2008), edited by Artimus Keiffer, provides useful insight into the state's early political development and settlement patterns.

While he never became president, Senator Robert A. Taft won the nickname "Mr. Republican," which provides the title of James T. Patterson's *Mr. Republican: A Biography of Robert A. Taft* (1972). *The Papers of Robert A. Taft*, a four-volume set released from 1997 to 2006 and edited by Clarence E. Wunderlin Jr., provide insight into Taft's thinking during his long career.

There are many books and articles on other important Ohio political figures that, while not tied directly to the state's presidential voting, are helpful in understanding the state. A sampling includes *Ohio's Kingmaker: Mark Hanna, Man and Myth* (2010) by William T. Horner; "Newton D. Baker: Cleveland's Greatest Mayor" by Thomas Suddes for Teaching Cleveland; *Politician Extraordinaire: The Tempestuous Life and Times of Martin L. Davey* (2008) by Frank P. Vazzano; *Frank J. Lausche: Ohio's Great Political Maverick* (2005) by James E. Odenkirk; *John J. Gilligan: The Politics of Principle* (2013) by Mark Bernstein; *Fighting the Unbeatable Foe: Howard Metzenbaum of Ohio, the Washington Years* (2008) by Tom Diemer; and *James A. Rhodes, Ohio Colossus* (2014) by Tom Diemer, Lee Leonard, and Richard Zimmerman. William Russell Coil provides an interesting look at Rhodes as a key figure in the GOP's efforts to win over blue collar workers in his 2005 Ohio State University doctoral dissertation, "'New Deal Republican': James Allen Rhodes and the Transformation of the Republican Party, 1933–1983."

While they are not specifically about Ohio, Sean Trende's *The Lost Majority: Why the Future of Government is Up for Grabs—and Who Will Take It* (2012), Morton Keller's *America's Three Regimes: A New Political History* (2007), and Colin Woodard's *American Nations: A History of the Eleven Rival Regional Cultures of North America* (2011) are all invaluable explorations of the nation's political and cultural development.

Finally, census and other demographic data from the mid-2010s come from *Profiles of Ohio* (2015). Historical census and demographic data come from the online resource Social Explorer, accessed through the University of Virginia libraries, as well as census documents maintained at the State Library of Ohio in Columbus.

Not all of the books and articles mentioned above are cited in this book, but they all helped inform the author's thinking on Ohio and its voting patterns.

# BIBLIOGRAPHY

Abramowitz, Alan, and Steven Webster. "All Politics Is National: The Rise of Negative Partisanship and the Nationalization of U.S. House and Senate Elections in the Twenty-First Century," paper presented at the Annual Meeting of the Midwest Political Science Association, Chicago, Illinois, April 16–19, 2015.

Barone, Michael. *Shaping Our Nation: How Surges of Migration Transformed America and Its Politics.* New York: Crown Forum, 2013.

Bernard, André, and Clifton Fadiman. *Bartlett's Book of Anecdotes.* Rev. ed. Boston: Little Brown and Company, 2000.

Bishop, Bill. *The Big Sort: Why the Clustering of Like-Minded America Is Tearing Us Apart.* New York: Mariner, 2009.

Campbell, David E., and J. Quin Monson. "The Religion Card: Gay Marriage and the 2004 Presidential Election." *Public Opinion Quarterly* 72, no. 3 (Fall 2008): 399–419.

Cayton, Andrew. *Ohio: The History of a People.* Columbus: Ohio State University Press, 2002.

Coffey, Daniel J., John C. Green, David B. Cohen, and Stephen C. Brooks. *Buckeye Battleground: Ohio, Campaigns, and Elections in the Twenty-First Century.* Akron: University of Akron Press, 2011.

Cooper, John Milton, Jr. *Woodrow Wilson: A Biography.* New York: Alfred A. Knopf, 2009.

Curtin, Michael F., and Joe Hallett. *The Ohio Politics Almanac.* 3rd rev. ed. Kent, OH: Kent State University Press, 2015.

Diemer, Tom, Lee Leonard, and Richard G. Zimmerman. *James A. Rhodes, Ohio Colossus.* Kent, OH: Kent State University Press, 2014.

Dudley, Robert L., and Ronald B. Rapoport. "Vice-Presidential Candidates and the Home State Advantage: Playing Second Banana at Home and On the Road." *American Journal of Political Science* 33, no. 2 (May 1989): 537–40.

Dunn, Susan. *1940: FDR, Willkie, Lindbergh, Hitler—the Election amid the Storm.* New Haven: Yale University Press, 2013.

Ellis, Richard J., and Mark Dedrick. "The Presidential Candidate, Then and Now." *Perspectives on Political Science* 26, no. 4 (Fall 1997): 208–16.

Fenton, John. *Midwest Politics.* New York: Holt, Rinehart and Winston, 1966.

Flinn, Thomas A. "Continuity and Change in Ohio Politics." *Journal of Politics* 24, no. 3 (August 1962): 521–44.

———. "How Mr. Nixon Took Ohio: A Short Reply to Senator Kennedy's Question." *Western Political Quarterly* 15, no. 2 (June 1962): 274–79.

Gerring, John. *Party Ideologies in America, 1828–1996.* New York: Cambridge University Press, 1998.

Goux, Darshan. "The Battleground State: Conceptualizing Geographic Contestation in American Presidential Elections, 1960–2004." PhD diss., University of California, Berkeley, 2010.

Gunther, John. *Inside U.S.A.* New York: Harper and Brothers, 1946.

Halberstam, David. *The Powers That Be.* Chicago: University of Illinois Press, 2000. First published 1979 by Alfred A. Knopf.

Hatcher, Harlan. *The Buckeye Country: A Pageant of Ohio.* New York: H. C. Kinsey, 1940.

Hecht, Stacey Hunter, and David Schultz, eds. *Presidential Swing States: Why Only Ten Matter.* Lanham, MD: Rowman and Littlefield, 2015.

Heidler, David S., and Jeanne T. Heidler. *Henry Clay: The Essential American.* New York: Random House, 2010.

Horner, William T. *Ohio's Kingmaker: Mark Hanna, Man and Myth.* Athens: Ohio University Press, 2010.

Howe, Henry. *Historical Collections of Ohio, vol. 2.* Norwalk, OH: State of Ohio/Laning Printing Company, 1896.

Inbody, Donald S. *The Soldier Vote: War, Politics, and the Ballot in America.* New York: Palgrave Macmillan, 2015.

Katznelson, Ira. *Fear Itself: The New Deal and the Origins of Our Time.* New York: Liveright, 2013.

Kennedy, David M. *Freedom from Fear: The American People in Depression and War, 1929–1945.* New York: Oxford University Press, 1999.

Kern, Kevin F., and Gregory S. Wilson. *Ohio: A History of the Buckeye State.* Chichester, UK: John Wiley, 2014.

Key, V. O., Jr. "A Theory of Critical Elections." *Journal of Politics* 17, no. 1 (February 1955): 3–18.

Knepper, George W. *Ohio and Its People.* 3rd ed. Kent, OH: Kent State University Press, 2003.

Lamis, Alexander P., and Brian Usher, eds. *Ohio Politics.* Rev. ed. Kent, OH: Kent State University Press, 2007.

Lazarsfeld, Paul F., Bernard R. Berelson, and Hazel Gaudet. *The People's Choice: How the Voter Makes Up His Mind in a Presidential Campaign.* New York: Duell, Sloan and Pearce, 1944.

Lubell, Samuel. *The Future of American Politics.* New York: Harper and Brothers, 1952.

————. "How Taft Did It." *Saturday Evening Post*, February 10, 1951.

————. "Post-Mortem: Who Elected Roosevelt?," *Saturday Evening Post*, January 25, 1941.

McPherson, James M. *Tried by War: Abraham Lincoln as Commander in Chief.* New York: Penguin, 2008.

Meinig, D. W. *The Shaping of America: A Geographical Perspective on 500 Years of History*, vol. 2, *Continental America 1800–1867.* New Haven: Yale University Press, 1993.

Ohio State Archaeological and Historical Society. *The American Guide Series: The Ohio Guide.* New York: Oxford University Press, 1943.

Parsons, Lynn Hudson. *The Birth of Modern Politics: Andrew Jackson, John Quincy Adams, and the Election of 1828.* New York: Oxford University Press, 2009.

Patterson, James T. *Grand Expectations: The United States, 1945–1974.* New York: Oxford University Press, 1996.

————. *Mr. Republican: A Biography of Robert A. Taft.* Boston: Houghton Mifflin, 1972.

Phillips, Kevin. *The Emerging Republican Majority.* Princeton: Princeton University Press, 2015. First published 1969 by Arlington House.

————. *The American Political Report* 6, no. 10, February 4, 1977.

Pomper, Gerald, ed. *The Election of 1988: Reports and Interpretations.* Chatham, NJ: Chatham House, 1989.

Roseboom, Eugene. *The History of the State of Ohio*, vol. 4, *The Civil War Era 1850–1873.* Columbus: Ohio State Archaeological and Historical Society, 1944.

Rosenstone, Steven J., Roy L. Behr, and Edward H. Lazarus. *Third Parties in America: Citizen Response to Major Party Failure.* 2nd ed. Princeton: Princeton University Press, 1996.

Sabato, Larry J. *The Kennedy Half Century: The Presidency, Assassination, and Lasting Legacy of John F. Kennedy.* New York: Bloomsbury, 2013.

Sabato, Larry J., Kyle Kondik, and Geoffrey Skelley, eds. *The Surge: 2014's Big GOP Win and What It Means for the Next Presidential Election.* Lanham, MD: Rowman and Littlefield, 2015.

Scammon, Richard M., and Ben J. Wattenberg. *The Real Majority: An Extraordinary Examination of the American Electorate.* New York: Coward, McCann and Geoghegan, 1970.

Smith, Daniel A., Matt DeSantis, and Jason Kassel. "Was Rove Right? Evangelicals and the Impact of Gay Marriage in the 2004 Election." Paper presented at the 5th Annual State Politics and Policy Conference, May 12–14, 2005, at Michigan State University.

Sternsher, Bernard. "The Harding and Bricker Revolutions: Party Systems and Voter Behavior in Northwest Ohio, 1860–1982." *Northwest Ohio Quarterly* 59, no. 3 (Summer 1987): 91–118.

Suddes, Thomas. "Newton D. Baker: Cleveland's Greatest Mayor." Teaching Cleveland.

Taft, Robert A. *The Papers of Robert A. Taft*, vol. 1, *1889–1938*. Edited by Clarence E. Wunderlin Jr. Kent, OH: Kent State University Press, 1997.

———. *The Papers of Robert A. Taft*, vol. 2, *1939–1944*. Edited by Clarence E. Wunderlin Jr. Kent, OH: Kent State University Press, 2001.

———. *The Papers of Robert A. Taft*, vol. 4, *1949–1953*. Edited by Clarence E. Wunderlin Jr. Kent, OH: Kent State University Press, 2006.

———. "How I Lost the Nomination." *Human Events*, December 2, 1959.

Trende, Sean. *The Lost Majority: Why the Future of Government Is Up for Grabs—and Who Will Take It*. New York: Palgrave Macmillan, 2012.

Tuchfarber, Alfred J. "Ohio: Presidential Politics in 'The Heart of It All.'" *Rothenberg Political Report* 5, no. 1 (Winter 1987–88): 15–18.

Tufte, Edward R., and Richard A. Sun. "Are There Bellwether Electoral Districts?" *Public Opinion Quarterly* 39, no. 1 (Spring 1975): 1–18. Available at http://www.edwardtufte.com/files/Bellwether3.pdf.

Weiss, Nancy J. *Farewell to the Party of Lincoln: Black Politics in the Age of FDR*. Princeton: Princeton University Press, 1983.

White, Theodore. *The Making of the President 1960*. New York: Atheneum, 1961.

Williams, R. Hal. *Realigning America: McKinley, Bryan, and the Remarkable Election of 1896*. Lawrence: University Press of Kansas, 2010.

Woodard, Colin. *American Nations: A History of the Eleven Rival Regional Cultures of North America*. New York: Viking Penguin, 2011.

# INDEX

Seltzer, Louis, 69
Shelby County, 60
Sherman, John, 45
Sherman, William Tecumseh, 45, 60
Sherman Anti-Trust Act, 45
Sherwin-Williams, 53
Silver, Nate, 79, 131
Smith, Al, 24, 69–70, 85, 87
Socialist Party, 65
Solid South, 29, 79
South Carolina, 15, 23, 29, 42
South Dakota, 91
Springsteen, Bruce, 39
Stark County, 66, 129; national attention as
    bellwether county, 115–17, 123
Stelter, Brian, 137
Sternsher, Bernard, 77
Steubenville, 73, 123
Stevenson, Adlai, 3, 11, 25, 84–85, 87
Stewart, Jimmy, 115
St. Louis, MO, 25
St. Paul, MN, 50
Strickland, Ted, 46–48
Suddes, Thomas, 47, 105
Sufferers' Lands, 39
Summit County, 66, 73, 75, 84, 90, 97, 123,
    125; political influence of KKK in, 70, 90
Summit County, UT, 116
Sun Belt, 132
Super PAC, 136
swing state, 19, 23, 41, 52, 107, 112, 133, 137;
    declining number of, 8; definition of and
    comparison to bellwether states, 2–6

Taft, Bob, 48, 106
Taft, Robert A., 48, 70, 75–78, 80, 82–83
Taft, Robert, Jr., 48, 88, 91
Taft, William Howard, 45–46, 64–65
Taylor, Paul, 107
Tea Party, 76
Tennessee, 15, 23, 42
Texas, 15, 23, 26, 40, 85, 93, 98, 100, 102, 137
Thurmond, Strom, 30, 54
Tidewater, 40, 42
Tilden, Samuel, 20
Toledo, 37, 64, 69, 85, 88, 91, 110, 124–25; 2008
    and 2012 African American voting in, 113
*Toledo Blade*, 89
TravelCenters of America, 53
Trende, Sean, 3, 6, 24, 32
Truman, Harry S., 2, 26, 30, 33, 80, 82–84
Trumbull County, 73, 125
Trump, Donald, 51–52, 99, 134

Tuchfarber, Al, 132
Tufte, Edward, 117
Tuscarawas County, 123
26th Amendment, 91–92

uniform swing, 129
Union County, 88, 128
Union Party (1864), 57
Union Party (1936), 77, 82
United States Election Project, 106
University of Akron Ray C. Bliss Institute of
    Applied Politics, 37
University of Michigan, 82, 92
US Constitution: 15th Amendment, 62; 26th
    Amendment, 91–92
Utah, 32, 116, 129, 137

Vallandigham, Clement, 56–58, 60, 113
Vaughn, Justin S., 45
Vermont, 6, 23–24, 42, 126, 136
Vinton County, 84
Virginia, 8, 10–11, 16, 23, 37, 42, 44, 93; trend
    toward Democrats, 133–34; and Virginia
    Military District, 39–40; voting similarly
    to Hamilton County, 123
Virginia Military District, 39–40, 90
Voinovich, George, 47, 49, 106

Wallace, George, 5, 9, 30, 54, 89–90, 99
Wallace, Henry, 82
Warren, Donald, 99
Warren, 73, 125
Warren County, 90, 110
Washington, DC, 133
*Washington Post*, 52, 99, 105, 128
Washtenaw County, MI, 91
Wayne County, 70
Wayne County, MI, 50
WBNS, 137
Weaver, James, 20
Webster, Steven, 14
Weiss, Nancy J., 71, 74
Western & Southern Financial Group, 54
Western Reserve, 39–40, 57, 65, 74; voting
    similarities to Connecticut, 43–44
West Virginia, 40; importance of coal
    industry in, 53; trend toward Republicans
    in, 103, 136
Wet (opponent of Prohibition), 69
Whig Party, 4–5, 44–45, 46, 94
White, Theodore, 7
Wilberforce University, 62
Willkie, Wendell, 76–77, 80, 117